# Windows® 8

## FOR

# DUMMIES®

## QUICK REFERENCE

# Windows® 8
## FOR
# DUMMIES®
## QUICK REFERENCE

by John Paul Mueller

WILEY

John Wiley & Sons, Inc.

**Windows® 8 For Dummies® Quick Reference**

Published by
**John Wiley & Sons, Inc.**
111 River Street
Hoboken, NJ 07030-5774

www.wiley.com

WILEY

# About the Author

**John Paul Mueller** is a freelance author and technical editor. He has writing in his blood, having produced 90 books and over 300 articles to date. The topics range from networking to artificial intelligence and from database management to heads-down programming. Some of his current books include Windows command-line references, books on VBA and Visio, several books on C#, and an IronPython programmer's guide. His technical editing skills have helped more than 63 authors refine the content of their manuscripts. John has provided technical editing services to both *Data Based Advisor* and *Coast Compute* magazines. He's also contributed articles to magazines such as *Software Quality Connection, DevSource, InformIT, SQL Server Professional, Visual C++ Developer, Hard Core Visual Basic, asp.netPRO, Software Test and Performance,* and *Visual Basic Developer.* Be sure to read John's blog at http://blog.johnmuellerbooks.com/.

When John isn't working at the computer, you can find him outside in the garden, cutting wood, or generally enjoying nature. John also likes making wine and knitting. When not occupied with anything else, he makes glycerin soap and candles, which comes in handy for gift baskets. You can reach John on the Internet at John@JohnMuellerBooks.com. John is also setting up a website at www.johnmuellerbooks.com/. Feel free to take a look and make suggestions on how he can improve it.

# Dedication

This book is dedicated to Smucker. Always the scamp, Smucker is the most loving of our four-legged kids and actually saved Rebecca's life once.

# Author's Acknowledgments

Thanks to my wife, Rebecca, for working with me to get this book completed. I really don't know what I would have done without her help in researching and compiling some of the information that appears in this book. She also did a fine job of proofreading my rough draft and helping me with the Glossary. Rebecca keeps the house running while I'm buried in work.

Russ Mullen deserves thanks for his technical edit of this book. He greatly added to the accuracy and depth of the material you see here. Russ is always providing me with great URLs for new products and ideas. However, it's the testing Russ does that helps most. He's the sanity check for my work. Russ also has different computer equipment than mine, so he's able to point out flaws that I might not otherwise notice.

Matt Wagner, my agent, deserves credit for helping me get the contract in the first place and taking care of all the details that most authors don't really consider. I always appreciate his assistance. It's good to know that someone wants to help.

A number of people read all or part of this book to help me refine the approach, test the coding examples, and generally provide input that all readers wish they could have. These unpaid volunteers helped in ways too numerous to mention here. I especially appreciate the efforts of Eva Beattie, Glenn Russell, and Hamid Ramazani, who provided general input, read the entire book, and selflessly devoted themselves to this project.

I especially appreciated the help I received from Lee Chantrey and the use of ViStart during the writing of this book. Lee was quite receptive to my input, and I can't wait to see the finished product.

Finally, I would like to thank Katie Feltman, Blair Pottenger, Becky Whitney, and the rest of the editorial and production staff at Wiley for their assistance in bringing this book to print. It's always nice to work with such a great group of professionals.

# Publisher's Acknowledgments

We're proud of this book; please send us your comments at `http://dummies.custhelp.com`. For other comments, please contact our Customer Care Department within the U.S. at 877-762-2974, outside the U.S. at 317-572-3993, or fax 317-572-4002.

Some of the people who helped bring this book to market include the following:

*Acquisitions and Editorial*

**Project Editor:** Blair J. Pottenger

**Senior Acquisitions Editor:** Katie Feltman

**Copy Editor:** Becky Whitney

**Technical Editor:** Russ Mullen

**Editorial Manager:** Kevin Kirschner

**Editorial Assistant:** Leslie Saxman

**Sr. Editorial Assistant:** Cherie Case

*Composition Services*

**Project Coordinator:** Katie Crocker

**Layout and Graphics:** Jennifer Creasey, Joyce Haughey, Christin Swinford

**Proofreaders:** ConText Editorial Services, Inc., John Greenough

**Indexer:** Valerie Haynes Perry

---

**Publishing and Editorial for Technology Dummies**

**Richard Swadley,** Vice President and Executive Group Publisher

**Andy Cummings,** Vice President and Publisher

**Mary Bednarek,** Executive Acquisitions Director

**Mary C. Corder,** Editorial Director

**Publishing for Consumer Dummies**

**Kathleen Nebenhaus,** Vice President and Executive Publisher

**Composition Services**

**Debbie Stailey,** Director of Composition Services

# Contents at a Glance

# Table of Contents

# Introduction

Microsoft has said that Windows 8 is "Windows reimagined." In fact, anyone who looks at Windows 8 for the first time will see something that looks completely different from anything Microsoft has done in the past. The fact is that Microsoft wants to provide an operating system that's simpler and more intuitive; one that works equally well on a desktop system and a tablet. *Windows 8 For Dummies Quick Reference* is designed as an aid to making it easier to work with Windows 8 — to make the differences easier to understand.

# About Windows 8 For Dummies Quick Reference

With all the changes you see, you might feel a little overwhelmed when you use Windows 8 at first. *Windows 8 For Dummies Quick Reference* is designed to provide you with assistance in performing common tasks. You use this book to quickly determine the exact set of steps you need to perform to move between the Start screen and the Desktop interface, or to access the Control Panel to make some much needed changes. The goal of this book isn't to teach you everything about Windows 8 — it's to make those tasks you perform every day a lot easier.

This book also focuses on reducing the learning curve for readers who've worked with Windows for years and now find themselves completely lost in a new environment. By using the tips and techniques in this book, you can get up and running with Windows 8 considerably faster than if you try hunting on your own for the features you need. Along the way, you discover some new features that Windows 8 provides to make your computing experience better, and you even get a glimpse of some nice-to-have features, such as the Windows Store.

# Foolish Assumptions

This book assumes that you're familiar with your system and that you've worked with Windows in the past. You won't find the hand-holding introductory information that a larger book provides. You aren't left out in the cold, either — every task is explained in detail, but my assumption is that you have

Windows experience. For example, you should know the basics of how to install, configure, and start an application. It's also a good idea to know how to use hardware features such as the touch system on your computer (assuming that you have a touch-enabled computer).

You definitely don't need to be an expert Windows user to benefit from this book. All the tasks are described using easily understandable, step-by-step procedures. A wealth of screen shots make it easy for you to see what your display should look like when you complete a task.

## Conventions Used in This Book

A few style conventions will help you navigate this book efficiently:

- ✔ Terms or words that I truly want to emphasize appear in *italics*. You can also find them defined in the Glossary, at the end of this book.

- ✔ Website addresses, or *URLs*, are shown like this: www.dummies.com.

- ✔ Numbered steps that you need to follow, and characters that you need to type (such as a user ID or a password) are set in **bold**.

## How This Book Is Organized

*Windows 8 For Dummies Quick Reference* is divided into ten parts. You don't have to read these parts sequentially, and you don't even have to read all the sections in any particular part. You can use the table of contents and the index to search for the information you need and quickly find your answer. This section provides a brief description of each part.

### The Big Picture: Windows 8

The Big Picture introduces Windows 8 to you. Consider this part an overview of what you can expect Windows 8 to provide. As with the rest of the book, you can find useful procedures for performing basic tasks in this part, but the emphasis is on providing an overview that helps you overcome some of the Windows 8 learning curve quickly.

## Part 1: Navigating the Start Screen

The biggest change in Windows 8 is its Start screen. What you see is a touch screen interface that's similar to those used by smartphones and tablets. However, the Start screen provides considerably more functionality, and this part of the book presents this functionality in a way that gets you started quickly. For example, you discover how to access the Control Panel when you need to make an adjustment to your system's configuration.

## Part 2: Navigating the Desktop Interface

All your Windows 7 applications should work just fine in Windows 8. However, getting to them is a bit different from the way you did it in the past. For one thing, you start on the Start screen and then must switch to the Desktop interface as needed to work with older applications. The Start menu is also missing, so you need to know how to work around that issue. This part of the book provides these bits of information and much more.

Many people are wary of the new Windows 8 setup and plan to spend most of their time working with the Desktop interface. If you fall into this category, you'll also want to read about ViStart, a Start menu replacement product, in this part. Using ViStart will make your Windows 8 computing experience a lot better if you plan to spend most of your time working with Desktop applications.

## Part 3: Using the Standard Applications

This part of the book helps you get your Desktop interface applications going. You'll see sections devoted to installation and configuration. One section tells you how to overcome compatibility issues in Windows 8. Even your Windows 7 applications can experience compatibility issues, so this particular section is especially important. You'll also see sections on performing tasks such as setting application security to ensure that the application can work as intended.

## Part 4: Working with Gadgets

*Gadgets* are small applications designed to sit on the Desktop and perform one or two tasks exceptionally well. This part of the book tells you about the gadgets found in Window 8, how to install and configure them, and how to obtain other gadgets, if you want them.

## Part 5: Using Internet Explorer

Microsoft is always adding new functionality to Internet Explorer. This part of the book discusses many of the new features found in the version of Internet Explorer that comes with Windows 8. You see how to configure Internet Explorer and how to work with the add-ons created for it. Most importantly, this part of the book describes all the new safety features that make your online computing experience safer.

## Part 6: Configuring Your System

Part 6 discusses many of the most common configuration tasks in Windows 8. One of the most important sections discusses how to ensure that all your devices work properly with Windows 8. You also find sections on working with themes, accessing the Control Panel, selecting a new power plan, and using the Windows 8 safety features, which are designed to protect your data.

## Part 7: Interacting with External Devices

Most people have external devices that they need to use with their systems. For example, you probably have a camera that you attach to the system in order to see the pictures it contains. This part of the book tells how to make these external devices work better with Windows 8.

## Part 8: Accessing the Network

Even home computers are networked today. This part provides pointers on making your network setup work better with Windows 8. Part 8 doesn't discuss networks in detail, but it provides enough information to overcome some of the most common hurdles that users have experienced.

## Part 9: Performing Administrative Tasks

All computers require a certain level of management by an administrator. Even if you own only one system and it isn't networked, you still need to perform administrative tasks to keep the computer running properly. This part discusses the most common administrative tasks that people need to perform when working with Windows 8.

# Icons Used in This Book

The familiar and helpful For Dummies icons point you in the direction of truly great information that's sure to help you as you look up information in the book. Look for these icons throughout *Windows 8 For Dummies Quick Reference*:

The Tip icon points out helpful information that's likely to make your job easier.

The Warning icon highlights lurking danger. When you see this icon, pay attention and proceed with caution.

# Windows 8

Windows 8 comes with an entirely new interface — one that will surprise many users with its ease of use. Microsoft's overriding goal in creating Windows 8 is to make the user interface easier to understand and more intuitive to use. This is also the first version of the operating system designed with tablet and phone users in mind. If you know how to perform a task on a phone or tablet, it's quite likely that you also know how to perform that task using Windows 8. The new Start screen provides a fully touch-interactive environment in which you can use the same gestures as you use for any of the smaller devices you own.

Of course, most people also need to perform tasks that rely on a more standard computer interface. With this in mind, you can also access the traditional Desktop interface and use it to work with applications such as Office or your organization's database application. The traditional Desktop interface also provides access to the same configuration and setup features you've used in the past. Administrators will still find all their favorite tools in Windows 8 and rely on the traditional Desktop interface to use them.

## In this part . . .

- ✔ **What You See**
- ✔ **Ribbon Toolbar**
- ✔ **Keyboard Shortcuts**
- ✔ **The Basics**
- ✔ **What You Can Do**

# What You See: The Start Screen

The following figure shows the Start screen as it might appear on your machine. Microsoft has made the Start screen extremely flexible, so you may see many of the same elements, but possibly in different locations. The Start screen uses some new technology, so this figure has labeled the new elements you need to know about. This terminology is used throughout the book, so be sure to pay close attention.

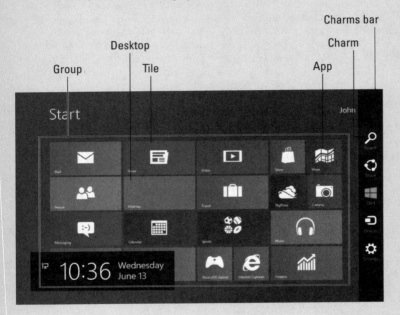

# What You See: The Desktop Interface

You already know about the Desktop interface from previous versions of Windows. The new Desktop interface for Windows 8 is notable in what it lacks. For example, you won't find the Start menu. Part 2 of this book describes a method for obtaining access to a Start menu you can use to speed your work. In the meantime, look at this version of the Desktop interface (the default Desktop is devoid of icons). Many of its elements are identified so that you know the terminology used throughout this book.

Desktop icons

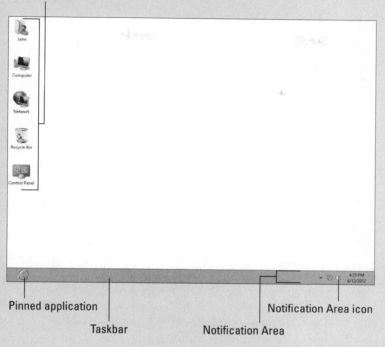

Pinned application

Taskbar

Notification Area icon

Notification Area

# *Ribbon Toolbar*

Most Windows 8 applications now use the Ribbon interface rather than the older menu-and-toolbar interface. The main reason for this change is that Microsoft has found that the Ribbon interface is more intuitive and easier for newer users to use. The application still has the same features, but the Ribbon rearranges them and presents them in a way that makes them easier to work with. Here's a typical example of the Ribbon interface with callouts for each major element.

Split button

Normal button    Split button with option selected

Tab                                Large button    Gallery

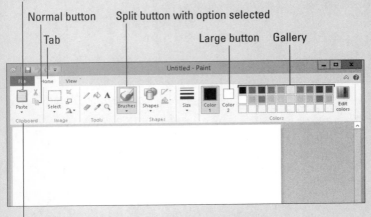

Group

TIP

The Ribbon provides a standard look across applications, and it won't surprise you to know that most applications have the same common tab elements, arranged in the same way. Seeing how to work with a single application helps you know what to expect in other applications that also rely on the Ribbon interface.

The most common tabs provided with applications are File, Home, and View. The following table contains a listing of the controls that you commonly find on these tabs and provides a short description of their use.

| Icon | Name | Tab | What It Does | Shortcut(s) |
|---|---|---|---|---|
| | New | File | Creates a new document. | Alt+F+N Ctrl+N |
| | Open | File | Opens a file for editing. | Alt+F+O Ctrl+O |
| | Save | File | Saves the file you have just edited. | Alt+F+S Ctrl+S |
| | Save As | File | Saves a file using a different name. | Alt+F+A F12 |
| | Print | File | Displays a menu of options for printing the document. | Alt+F+P Ctrl+P |
| | Properties | File | Displays a dialog box containing options for configuring the application. | Alt+F+E Ctrl+E |

| Icon | Name | Tab | What It Does | Shortcut(s) |
|---|---|---|---|---|
| About | About | File | Tells you about the application. | Alt+F+T |
| Exit | Exit | File | Ends the current application session. | Alt+F+X |
| Paste | Paste | Home | Pastes the data found on the Clipboard into the current document. | Alt+H+V<br>Ctrl+V |
| Cut | Cut | Home | Cuts the selection from the document and places it on the Clipboard. | Alt+H+X<br>Ctrl+X |
| Copy | Copy | Home | Copies the selection and places it on the Clipboard. | Alt+H+C<br>Ctrl+C |
| Zoom in | Zoom in | View | Displays a larger image of the document with less content. | Alt+V+I<br>Ctrl+PgUp |
| Zoom out | Zoom out | View | Displays a smaller image of the document with more content. | Alt+V+O<br>Ctrl+PgDn |
| 100% | 100% | View | Displays the document at 100 percent of its normal size. | Alt+V+M |
| Rulers | Rulers | View | Displays rules along the top and side of the editing area to make it easier to measure items in the document. | Alt+V+R<br>Ctrl+R |
| Gridlines | Gridlines | View | Displays a grid to make it easier to align document items. | Alt+V+G<br>Ctrl+G |
| Status bar | Status bar | View | Displays status information on a bar at the bottom of the application. | Alt+V+S |

Many users find that the Ribbon takes up too much space. You can hide (minimize) the Ribbon by pressing Ctrl+F1, and you can display (expand) it again by pressing Ctrl+F1 a second time. (Other existing tricks, such as double-clicking a tab to minimize or maximize the Ribbon, still work, too.) Moving the mouse up toward the Ribbon temporarily expands it, so you can keep the Ribbon minimized and access its features only when needed.

# Keyboard Shortcuts

Using keyboard shortcuts can make accessing Windows 8 features faster and easier, in some cases, especially if you're a touch typist. Every version of Windows has had its own unique set of special keyboard shortcuts, and Windows 8 is no different. Besides common keyboard shortcuts, such as Ctrl+V to paste content from the Clipboard to the current application, Windows 8 supports the unique keyboard shortcuts shown in the following table that will improve your computing experience.

| Shortcut | What It Does |
|---|---|
| Win | Displays the Start screen. |
| Win+C | Opens the Charms bar. |
| Win+D | Shows the Desktop interface. |
| Win+E | Opens File Explorer. |
| Win+F | Opens the Search pane so that you can look for files. |
| Win+H | Opens the Share charm. |
| Win+I | Opens the Settings charm. |
| Win+K | Opens the Connect charm. |
| Win+L | Locks the computer. |
| Win+M | Minimizes all applications in the Desktop interface. |
| Win+O | Locks the screen rotation. |
| Win+P | Lets you select from a list of available displays when working with a multimonitor system. |
| Win+Q | Opens the Search pane so that you can look for applications. |
| Win+R | Opens the Run dialog box. |
| Win+U | Open the Ease of Access Center. |
| Win+V | Cycles through *toasts,* which are notifications that your application can display when something has happened and the application isn't viewable. |
| Win+Shift+V | Reverse-cycles through toasts. |
| Win+W | Opens the Search pane so that you can look for settings. |
| Win+X | Launches the Start menu (a list of actions you can perform). |
| Win+Z | Displays the *App bar,* which is a special area at the bottom of the Start screen that holds application settings. |
| Win+Spacebar | Changes the language selection and keyboard layout. |
| Win+Enter | Launches the Narrator. |
| Win+PgUp | Moves tiles to the left. |

| Shortcut | What It Does |
|---|---|
| Win+PgDn | Moves tiles to the right. |
| Win+Tab | Cycles through the list of running apps, including Windows 8 apps on the Start screen. |
| Win+Shift+Tab | Cycles through the list of running apps in reverse order. |
| Win+. | Moves the split between groups to the right. |
| Win+Shift+. | Moves the split between groups to the left. |
| Win+, | Lets you peek at the desktop. |
| Ctrl+Tab | Displays a list of all available apps when working on the Start screen. |

# The Basics: Accessing a Windows 8 App on the Start Screen

For anyone who has long used Windows applications, Windows 8 apps on the Start screen require a somewhat different approach because they work differently. When you click a Windows 8 app tile to start the application, it runs until Windows decides that you aren't using it. You don't actually stop the Windows 8 app.

Windows 8 apps always run in full-screen view. You don't generally see multiple applications at the same time.

When a developer designs a Windows 8 app, it can run equally well on any screen size. The same Windows 8 app runs on a smartphone, tablet, laptop, or desktop system. Though the various devices may not access the same amount of information, the application automatically sizes itself to meet the requirements of the particular device.

In most cases, the control system for a Windows 8 app is small. You don't see long lists of options, menus, or other items that you may be used to seeing in your Windows environment. Some Windows 8 apps may not even have much of a control system — a simple click here or there is all you can do. The following sections discuss a typical Windows 8 app in two ways: at the interface level and within the application itself.

## Interacting with an application using the App bar

The Start screen presents the list of apps as tiles within a group. You can select a specific app using the mouse or the arrow keys. Press Enter to start the app, or press the Spacebar to interact with it. When you press the Spacebar, you see the App bar as shown.

App bar

Different apps support different App bar features. In this case, you can perform four different tasks. The following list describes the most common actions you can perform using the App bar:

- ✔ **Unpin from Start:** The application is removed from Start. However, the application is still available when you look for it in the list of all applications. If you later decide that you want quick access to this app, you can pin it on Start again.

- ✔ **Uninstall:** Windows uninstalls the app and makes it unavailable. You don't see it in the listing of all apps, either. To access the app again, you must reinstall it.

- ✔ **Smaller:** Tiles come in different sizes. If you don't use an app often, you can make its tile smaller so that it uses less screen "real estate."

- ✔ **Turn Live Tile On:** The Live Tile feature can display a small version of what the app is doing in the background. Turning on this feature would show you the latest news or weather, as an example. If the app isn't doing anything, you see a static display of the latest content. When an application does perform an update, it uses the same network bandwidth as usual, so you'll want to turn this feature off when network bandwidth is at a premium.

- ✔ **Clear Selection:** If you select multiple tiles, you can choose to clear a selection, which means that it's no longer part of the group you're working.

- **Open New Window (Desktop applications only):** A new copy of the application opens in a separate window.

- **Run as Administrator (Desktop applications only):** To gain the rights required by the application, you may have to run it using administrator credentials. Windows may ask you to provide an appropriate username and password to use this feature.

- **Open File Location (Desktop applications only):** This feature starts the application and sends it the name of a file that you want to open. You see the file opened in the application as soon as it starts.

- **Pin (or Unpin) from Taskbar (Desktop applications only):** In addition to pinning the application to Start so that you can access it from the Start screen, you can pin it to the Taskbar so that you can access it from the Desktop interface.

- **All Apps:** Display a list of every installed app on your system. You can use this display to interact with apps much as you would when working with Start. This includes pinning the application to Start or to the Taskbar (for applications that run in the Desktop interface).

## Interacting with an application's controls

After you start a Windows 8 app, you see a full-screen view of it. A scroll bar lets you move left or right to access other features of the application. If you don't see the scroll bar, simply move the mouse down to the bottom of the display.

 When Windows displays the scroll bar, you see the Minus (–) button on the right side of the display. Click this button to see a list of app features. Click a feature and you'll see that feature displayed onscreen.

Right-clicking anywhere in the display shows the App bar, containing settings for the application. Most applications have the App bar appear at the top of the display, some show it at the bottom of the display, and some have both, as shown for the Weather app.

In this case, the controls at the top let you choose the location you want to see. The Home button displays the default weather location you choose. Places displays a list of locations you configure for the app. When you want to see the weather in general, click World Weather.

The lower App bar displays a list of actions you can perform with the current location. For example, you can choose to remove this location from your list of places or set it as your default location. Click Pin to Start to pin this particular location to Start so that you can access it immediately and see updates as they occur using the Live Tile feature. The app defaults to using the unit of measure for your location (Fahrenheit, for the United States). You can choose to use Celsius instead. The app also provides automatic updates, but you can choose to refresh the information manually whenever you want.

# The Basics: Moving Between the Start Screen and the Desktop

Windows 8 provides a number of methods for moving between the Start screen and the Desktop interface. The following list describes the methods you use most often:

- Click the Desktop tile.
- Press Win+D.
- Click an app tile that uses the Desktop (such as Calculator or Notepad).
- Press Win+C to display the Charms bar and then click the Start charm.
- Press Win+F to display the Files Search pane, locate a file that requires a Desktop application, and click that file.
- Press Win+Q to display the Apps Search pane, locate an application that requires the Desktop interface, and click that application.

# The Basics: Accessing a Traditional Windows Application

The default Desktop interface presentation is devoid of icons, except for having Internet Explorer pinned to the Taskbar. Therefore, you can always access Internet Explorer by clicking its icon. In addition, you'll find no Start menu of the sort found in older versions of Windows. (The "Restoring the Start Menu" section in Part II shows how to install a third-party Start menu alternative.)

When you want to access other Desktop applications, you must configure the Desktop interface to support them or provide another means of accessing them. The following sections describe three common methods for accessing traditional Windows applications using the Desktop interface with no form of third-party Start menu support.

## Pinning applications to the Taskbar

The applications you use most often are easily accessible when you place them on the Taskbar. Just as Internet Explorer is pinned to the Taskbar, you can pin any other application that you need to access often. The following steps describe how to pin a Desktop application to the Taskbar when starting on the Start screen:

1. **Press Win+Z to display the App bar.**

   You see the App bar appear at the bottom of the Start screen.

2. **Click All Apps.**

   You see a listing of all of the applications on your system, as shown here. (The Start screen scrolls left and right, versus up and down, so you scroll left to see the other icons shown in this screen shot.)

3. **Right-click the application you want to pin to the Taskbar.**

   In this case, the example uses Calculator, but this technique works equally well for every other Desktop application. Windows displays the App bar at the bottom of the display, as shown here.

4. **Click Pin to Taskbar.**

   Windows pins the application to the Taskbar. The application automatically appears on the Taskbar the next time you open the Desktop interface.

## Using the Run dialog box

Use the Run dialog box to access applications that you use less often. The Run dialog box can accept these elements:

- An application's executable name
- The human-readable name of the application, such as Outlook or Notepad
- The name of a file associated with a particular application

To open an application using this technique, press Win+R to display the Run dialog box. Type the name of the application or associated file that you want to open in the Open field and then click OK. Here's how the Run dialog box would look if you wanted to open Notepad.

Click Browse in the Run dialog box when you don't remember the name of the application or associated file that you want to open. You see the Browse dialog box, which you can use to locate the resource on disk.

## Placing applications on the Desktop

As an alternative to pinning applications to the Taskbar, you can create shortcuts to applications on the Desktop. In fact, Windows uses this approach for providing access to these default features:

- ✔ Computer
- ✔ User's files
- ✔ Network
- ✔ Recycle Bin
- ✔ Control Panel

Use the following procedure to place the standard icons on the Desktop:

1. **Right-click the Desktop and choose Personalize from the context menu.**

   You see the Personalization window, shown here.

   ![Personalization window screenshot]

2. **Click Change Desktop Icons.**

   You see the Desktop Icon Settings dialog box, shown here.

3. **Select the icons you want to work with and click OK.**

Windows adds the icons you requested to the Desktop.

When working with applications, folders, or files, all you need to do is right-click the item you want to place on the Desktop and then choose Copy from the context menu. Next, right-click the Desktop and choose Copy Shortcut from the context menu. Windows creates the shortcut you requested, and you can access the resource.

# What You Can Do: Using a Local Account

When you install Windows 8, it forces you to use a remote account — one that's based on your Windows Live ID. A remote account works fine for interacting with the Start screen. In fact, you need it in order to perform certain tasks with Windows 8 apps, such as accessing a SkyDrive. However, the remote account doesn't allow you to perform certain tasks that Desktop users need to perform, such as working with the features of the Computer Management folder.

Your remote account (the one that uses the Windows Live ID) is always accessible from your local account, but your local account is never accessible from your remote account. To perform all the tasks listed in this book, you need a local account — one that has full access to your system and your network connections. The following procedure shows how to create a local account using the Start screen.

# The Big Picture: Windows 8

1. **Press Win+C.**

   You see the Charms bar appear.

2. **Click the Settings charm.**

   Windows displays the Settings panel, shown here.

3. **Click Change PC Settings at the bottom of the Settings panel.**

   You see the PC Settings charm, shown here.

4. **Click Add a User.**

*BP-22*

Windows displays the Add a User Wizard, as shown here. Notice that there doesn't appear to be any way to create a local account, though Step 5 fixes this problem.

5. **Click Sign In Without a Microsoft Account.**

   The wizard changes to include a new button, Local Account.

6. **Click Local Account.**

   The Add a User Wizard asks for the specific user account information, as shown here. Provide your standard user account information for your organization so that you have full access to all the functionality you normally have with your account. If you're lacking any of this information, ask your administrator for help.

7. **Fill in the local user information and click Next.**

   You see the new user's information onscreen.

8. **Click Finish.**

   The local account is ready for use.

 The remainder of this book assumes that you're using a local account to ensure maximum Windows functionality, so you have to log in to your remote account at times to perform Start screen–specific tasks. The procedures always tell you when a remote login is required.

# What You Can Do: Visiting the Windows Store

The Windows Store is one of the Windows 8 apps that most people will likely use at some point. The term *store* is a bit of a misnomer because you can find both paid and free items there. At the Windows Store, you can obtain Windows 8 apps to use with Windows 8.

To work with the Windows Store, all you need to do is click the Store tile (the one with the Shopping Bag icon). You see the Windows Store appear. Here's an example of what you might see:

As with any store, this one has departments. You can simply scroll through the departments by using the scroll wheel on your mouse or pressing Win+PgDn and Win+PgUp to move back and forth. Free products have the word *Free* displayed in the lower-left corner of the tile, while paid products will display pricing information. The bottom of the tile has a rating for the particular application.

To install any of these applications, simply click its tile. You see a description of the application. On the left side of the display is the Install button, as shown in the figure. Clicking the button installs the application on your machine.

When you click Install using a local account, Windows asks for your Windows Live ID (your remote account credentials). You can't get items from the Windows Store without this information. Here's what you typically see after clicking Install:

Immediately after you enter your credentials, it appears that something has failed because you return to the Windows Store. Don't worry: The app is installing in the background. If you look at the Start screen, you see the app's tile with the word *Installing* in the lower-left corner, as shown in the figure. When this process is complete, a pop-up message appears telling you that the app is ready for use.

The Windows Store includes all sorts of applications that you can use with Windows 8 — everything from games to productivity apps. It even has Windows 8 tools, business apps, and apps to secure your system, so take time to explore the Windows Store for the Windows 8 apps you need.

# What You Can Do: Shutting Down Your System

It's the end of the day and you want to shut down your system before you go home. When working with previous versions of Windows, you could open the Start menu and select the proper option for shutting down your system. Windows 8 doesn't appear to provide this option — at least, not where you can see it.

Windows 8 has a few other options, not discussed in this book, for shutting down your system. For example, you can open an administrative command prompt and use the Shutdown command. The following sections describe how to shut down your system from both the Start screen and Desktop interface.

## Using the Start screen

The Start screen provides a quick method of shutting down your system. The following steps assume that you're starting on the Start screen:

1. **Press Win+C.**

   You see the Charms bar appear.

2. **Click the Settings charm.**

   Windows displays the Settings panel.

3. **Click Power.**

   Windows presents options for Sleep, Shutdown, and Restart.

4. **Click Shutdown.**

   Your system closes all its applications and shuts down normally.

## Using the Desktop interface

Windows 8 has no direct method for shutting down the system from the Desktop interface. In this case, the fastest way to shut down your system is to press Ctrl+Alt+Delete. You see a menu with options for signing out of the system and starting the Task Manager (among other options). In the lower-right corner, you see the Power icon, where you can choose to shut down your system.

# Part 1

# Navigating the Start Screen

The *Start screen* presents Microsoft's new method of providing apps to users. It uses a different approach for interacting with the user, one that's supposed to be easier and more straightforward than traditional Windows applications of the past. The idea is that you should be able to sit down with a Windows 8 app and use it immediately without resorting to Help much (if at all). In short, Windows 8 apps are supposed to be more intuitive and simpler to use.

This part explores Windows 8 apps using five Microsoft-specified tenets as guidelines. You'll discover how the new Start screen differs from the traditional Windows Desktop interface that you've used in the past.

## In this part . . .

✔ **Defining a Windows 8 App**

✔ **Employing the Start Screen**

✔ **Interacting with the App Bar**

✔ **Using Charms**

✔ **Using Location Data**

# Defining a Windows 8 App

Window 8 apps are different from Windows applications because Microsoft holds them to a stricter standard. Microsoft has specified that a Windows 8 app must uphold/adhere to all five of these tenets:

- **Show pride in craftsmanship:** To improve the quality of the application you receive, Microsoft is monitoring the kinds of applications that developers put together. The user experience must be complete and polished at every stage.

- **Be fast and fluid:** Microsoft has placed new emphasis on direct interaction with content and making this experience as seamless as possible. The app should actually tell a story using motion (meaning that Windows 8 apps should be more interactive).

- **Be authentically digital:** Windows 8 apps make optimal use of the digital medium — to provide the end user with an experience that goes beyond the real-world experience by using bright colors and images.

- **Do more with less:** The app shouldn't present any sort of distraction to working with content. In short, the user should be able to focus on content without even seeing the application. Microsoft seems to want a spartan application interface with a minimum of controls.

- **Win as one:** An app should be able to work with all devices and other apps, as well as with the host system, no matter which platform is in use. In short, an app should work equally well on mobile devices, laptops, and PCs.

# Employing the Start Screen

The *Start screen* is the focal point of the Windows 8. Given the five tenets that Microsoft has applied to Windows 8 apps (see the previous section), the Start screen is simple to use, and it focuses on content and provides "motion" in the form of Live Tiles. (A Live Tile provides the means to see changing information from any source designed to provide it at a glance. You need to have access to that information source, such as through an Internet connection, for the Live Tile to work. For example, you can see updates of the news and current weather in miniature in a single glance.) The following sections describe how to use the Start screen to access Windows 8 apps in more detail.

## Accessing apps

In The Big Picture, you see that you can start a Windows 8 app by simply clicking it. The app always opens in full-screen mode, which means that you see only that app presented onscreen. The focus is on content, so you don't even see any controls in many cases. The app can contain multiple panels, each of which contains specific content. Clicking an element within the content can display additional information when it's available. For example, in the News app presentation shown in Figure 1-1, each tile presents a different story. Clicking a tile displays specifics about that story. You don't need any controls because the interface is simple enough to work without them.

**Figure 1-1**

Tile size is important. The large tile about President Obama is the main story of the day. Lesser stories use smaller blocks to reduce their emphasis. Most Windows 8 apps rely on this technique to make it easy for you to pick out the most significant or compelling content quickly. This app can also rely on Live Tiles (even though you obviously can't see them in action in this book) so that you can detect changes in stories without taking the time to open them.

Right-clicking the display presents the App bar in the application. When you right-click the News app, the App bar contains options for moving to different news focuses. (See Figure 1-2.) For example, click My News and you'll see a series of stories specifically tailored to address the kinds of content you request by specifying keywords. Click Sources and you'll see news stories from each newswire or publisher.

App bar

**Figure 1-2**

Every Windows 8 app also has access to the Charms bar. Simply press Win+C to display it. You can also move the mouse cursor toward the right side of the display or swipe the right side of the display when using a touch interface. The Charms bar will contain the same charms as normal. (See Figure 1-3.) However, some charms, such as Settings, will contain options specifically for the app in use. For example, click Rate and Review on the Settings charm to rate the News app.

A Windows 8 app provides you with the functionality needed to work with content, but with the rights of the content provider in mind. For example, you may click a story heading, press Win+C to display the Charms bar, and then click Share to share the story with someone else. If the content provider has protected the story, you see a simple message saying that you can't share the content, as shown in Figure 1-4.

When an app supports sharing, you see the appropriate sharing options for that app. For example, you may be looking at a game app in the Windows Store and want to share that information with someone else. You can send the information using e-mail, or you can send it directly to someone on your contacts list, as shown in Figure 1-5.

Charms bar

**Figure 1-3**

**Figure 1-4**

**Figure 1-5**

You don't have to think about what you can do because the app makes the options obvious. The number of controls in each app — when controls are necessary — is limited. In addition, every app supports both the App bar and the Charms bar. The Charms bar always contains the same charms, and the App bar contains controls for app-specific settings that you can change when needed.

## Zooming in and out

All Windows 8 apps support zooming. This feature may not be useful in a game, but every app supports it. Either an app is zoomed or not zoomed — an app can't support multiple levels of zoom. When you have the app zoomed, you see an overview of what the app has to offer. Otherwise, you see the specific content you requested.

To zoom an app, place the mouse in the lower-right corner of the display (or swipe in that location when using a touch interface). You see the minus (–) sign in a square block. Click the minus sign to zoom the app. For example, Figure 1-6 shows what the News app looks like when zoomed.

**Figure 1-6**

The display shows several categories of news. The main story in each category appears as a Live Tile in that category's tile. Select a specific category of news by clicking the tile you want. The stories in that category appear so that you can see them and choose a story to read.

# Interacting with the App Bar

The *App bar* is an essential part of the Start screen experience. Individual Windows 8 apps use the App bar to allow you to make changes to the application's settings or choose the kind of content you want. The App bar also makes it possible to choose different content areas and to customize the content to meet your needs. However, you won't find controls in the sense that traditional Windows applications use controls. The App bar is focused on content, and it helps determine how to manipulate content to suit your needs.

The Start screen is a kind of application, so it too has the App bar. Just as the App bar in the apps mentioned earlier in this part vary their content to meet specific needs, so does the App bar on the Start screen. The Big Picture shows you how to perform tasks using the App bar. The following sections refine that information.

## Accessing all the applications

No matter what you're doing at the Start screen, you can always access all registered applications on a system. *Registered* applications install themselves in Windows. If an application simply resides on the hard drive and you didn't perform an installation for it, the application doesn't appear as part of the Apps list by default.

To display the list of all applications, right-click the Start screen, press Win+Z, or swipe at the bottom of the display to display the App bar. Click All Apps and you'll see the Apps screen. Windows 8 apps appear first in the list. Desktop applications, including Windows utilities, appear within groups after the Windows 8 apps, as shown in Figure 1-7 (your display may look slightly different than the one shown).

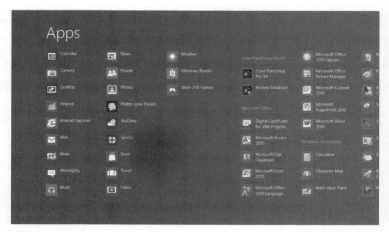

**Figure 1-7**

To select an app (or multiple apps) for configuration, right-click its tile in the list. A check mark appears in the upper-right corner of the selected tile. The information you see on the App bar after selecting a tile depends on the application type. Windows 8 apps provide the fewest options, as shown in Figure 1-8.

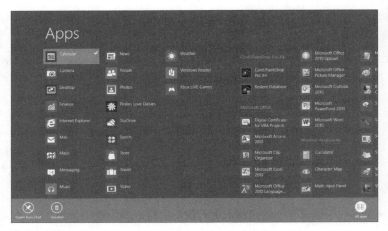

**Figure 1-8**

Desktop applications present more options because you can configure them in a number of ways. For example, you can't pin a Windows 8 app to the Taskbar, but you can pin a Desktop application to the Taskbar. Windows 8 apps load with the content that you'll see when using them. Desktop applications can work with different files, so you can choose to start the Desktop application with a particular file. Figure 1-9 shows the typical set of options for a Desktop application.

**Figure 1-9**

## Altering the Start screen

The Start screen that Microsoft creates for you when you install Windows 8 is only a starting point. You should modify the Start screen to meet your specific needs. If you find that you aren't using the Weather app, for example, remove it from the Start screen. On the other hand, if you find that you need nearly constant access to the Calculator, feel free to add it to the Start screen. With this in mind, your Start screen may not match the one you see in the figures throughout this book because you'll make plenty of changes to it. The following sections describe methods you can use to change the Start screen.

### Pinning or unpinning an app

When you *pin* an app, you place it on either the Start screen or the Taskbar (in the Desktop interface). Pinning an app is the easiest and fastest way to make the apps you use most often easily accessible. When you *unpin* an app, you remove it from either the Start screen or the Taskbar. The app is still available, but you need to go to the Apps screen to see it. (See the "Accessing all the applications" section, earlier in this part, for details.)

Pin apps to the Start screen or Taskbar carefully. Many users have the urge to pin every app they'll ever use to the Start screen or Taskbar (or possibly both). The more apps you pin, the more apps you have to look through before starting the application. At some point, the technique that you thought would increase your efficiency ends up slowing you down because you have too many items.

When you want to make an app readily available for use, you pin it to the Start screen. Use these steps to pin an app to the Start screen:

1.  **Press Win+Z or right-click the Start screen to display the App bar.**

    You see the Apps screen.

2.  **Right-click the app you want to pin to the Start screen.**

    You see the App bar showing the options for that app. Figure 1-10 shows what the App bar looks like in the Windows Reader app.

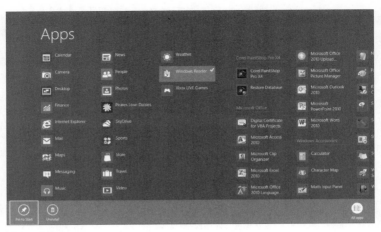

**Figure 1-10**

There are many ways to right-click an app. For example, you can use the arrow keys to select it and then press the spacebar. To right-click a touch screen, press your finger on the screen and hold it there until you see the right-click result.

3. **Click the Pin to Start option.**

Windows adds the application to the Start screen.

To select the Pin to Start option by using keyboard commands, press Tab to select the App bar, use the arrow keys to select Pin to Start, and then press Enter.

You can unpin any app that's pinned to the Start screen. Use these steps to unpin an app:

1. **Right-click the app you want to unpin from the Start screen.**

You see the App bar for that app.

2. **Click the Unpin from Start option.**

Windows removes the app tile from the Start screen.

### Uninstalling an app

Pinning and unpinning apps either makes them more visible or hides them from view. However, even if the app isn't pinned, it's still present on your machine. To remove an app permanently so that no one can access it, you must uninstall it. Use the following steps to uninstall an app:

1. **Right-click the app you want to uninstall.**

   You see the App bar showing the options for that app.

2. **Click the Uninstall option.**

   Windows immediately returns you to the Apps screen and starts uninstalling the app in the background. You see a *toast* message (a brief, onscreen notification that the uninstall is complete) when Windows completes the process.

### Making an app tile smaller or larger

An app tile can appear in one of two different sizes on the Start screen. Use large tiles for apps that you use often or that have live feeds you need to view. Small tiles make apps accessible, but in a smaller space. The following steps tell how to make an app tile smaller or larger:

1. **Right-click the app tile you want to resize.**

   You see the App bar showing the options for that app.

2. **Click Smaller (to make the tile smaller) or Larger (to make the tile larger).**

   Windows resizes the app tile and moves the remaining tiles to accommodate the change.

### Moving an app tile

Presenting app tiles in the right order can make it easier for you to find the app you want to use. To move an app tile, simply click and drag it to a new location. If you want to use the keyboard, highlight the tile you want to move and then press Alt+*arrow key* (where *arrow key* is the direction you want to move the tile: up, down, left, or right).

### Turning Live Tiles on or off

Live Tiles display information as it changes in an app. You use Live Tiles to see the current app state (such as the status of a paused game) or to monitor the app for a particular change (such as news updates). However, having too many Live Tiles can prove distracting and also use valuable processing cycles on your system, so be sure to use Live Tiles only as needed.

Only certain apps support Live Tiles. The following steps show how to turn Live Tile support on or off:

1. **Right-click the app tile you want to modify.**

   You see the App bar showing the options for that app.

2. **Click Turn Live Tile On or Turn Live Tile Off.**

   Windows modifies the Live Tile status for the selected tile.

## Creating a new group

Groups help you organize tiles into a usable form. A *group* is an associated set of tiles. For example, you might want to create a group for games and another group for business apps you use every day. Another group can contain utilities you use often enough to place them on the Start screen, but not often enough to keep them with your business apps. Windows separates each group by a space, as shown in the zoomed view in Figure 1-11 (groups are used in both zoomed and unzoomed views, but are easier to see when you zoom the screen).

Space separating the groups

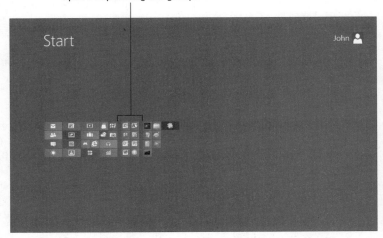

**Figure 1-11**

Figure 1-11 shows three groups: The first contains the standard Windows 8 apps, the second contains Office applications, and the third contains utilities. To create a fourth group — one for games — you drag the first game outside the group it resides in. This action creates a new group containing only that tile.

To add new tiles to this group, drag the tile so that it touches the first tile. The two tiles become part of the same group.

## Displaying the administrative tools

*Administrative* tools are specialized utilities used to manage the Windows 8 setup. For example, when you want to manage the printers on a system, you need access to the administrative tools.

The administrative tools are potentially dangerous. Misusing them can damage your Windows 8 setup. If you aren't sure whether you should work with the administrative tools, you probably shouldn't attempt to gain access to them. You must also have the proper rights to use these tools. When you try to use a tool that you shouldn't access, Windows displays the "Access Denied" error message.

Obtaining access to the administrative tools is one reason why you need a local account in Windows 8. Because a remote account presents potential security issues, Windows 8 locks access to some of the administrative tools, even if you have an administrator account. Even elevating your account security by using the Run As Administrator option doesn't unlock these applications because using them with a remote account is dangerous.

All the administrative tools are still accessible by using the Administrative Tools folder of the Control Panel. As with any version of Windows, you must have administrator privileges for the system in order to access most of these features. (If any of this information sounds mysterious, you really don't need it.) The following steps show how to add administrative tools access to the Start screen:

*1.* **Press Win+C.**

   You see the Charms bar.

*2.* **Click Settings.**

   You see the Settings panel, as shown in Figure 1-12.

**Figure 1-12**

3. **Click Tiles.**

You see the Tiles panel, as shown in Figure 1-13.

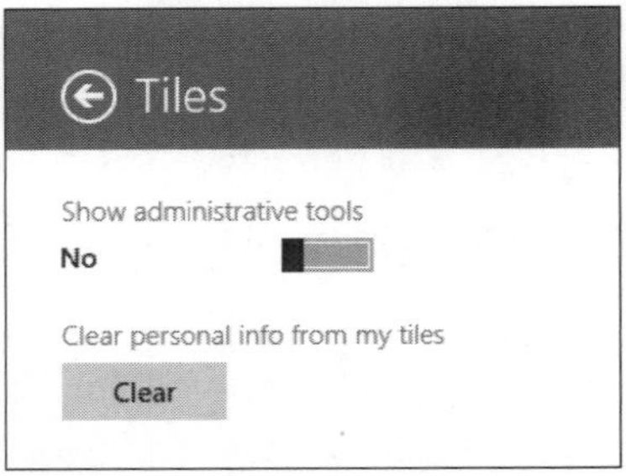

**Figure 1-13**

**4. Click the Show Administrative Tools switch.**

The switch moves into the On position. Windows adds the administrative tools to the Start screen. Figure 1-14 shows a typical example of what you see. The two groups on the right hold the administrative tools.

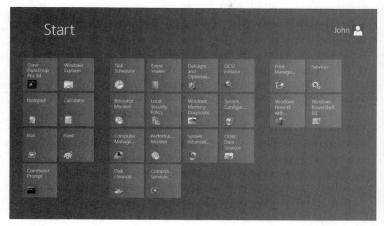

**Figure 1-14**

You can turn off the Show Administrative Tools switch if you decide that you don't want the administrative tools tiles added to the Start screen. As with any other tile, you can move these tiles, create special groups with them, or hide the ones you don't use.

## Removing personal information

People have many concerns about privacy issues on the Internet, and for good reason — you read about a new privacy breach almost every day in the news. With this in mind, it's possible to clear the personal information used by Windows 8 apps. The app may require reconfiguration the next time you use it, but your identity will be safer. The following steps describe how to clear personal information from Windows 8 tiles:

**1. Press Win+C.**

You see the Charms bar.

**2. Click Settings.**

You see the Settings panel.

3. **Click Tiles.**

   You see the Tiles panel.

4. **Click Clear under the Clear Personal Info from My Tiles heading.**

   Windows clears any personal information found within the tiles.

 Personal information appears in many places on your machine. For example, the browser you use probably contains personal information in the form of cookies and other data stored on your hard drive. The previous steps clear only the *tile* information, not any other source of personal information on your machine. You must clear information from other sources to ensure complete system security.

# Using Charms

The Charms bar contains five charms: Search, Share, Start, Devices, and Settings. These charms are always accessible, and they help you configure the system and apps while you work in the Start screen. In some cases, charms include contextual settings. For example, the Settings charm often contains special settings for the app you're using. The following sections describe the common features of each charm that Windows 8 supports. In later parts of this book, you encounter some app-specific settings information.

## Using the Search charm

Microsoft has worked hard to continue improving the search capability of Windows over the years. You can search content in a wealth of ways in Windows 8. However, the emphasis in this version of Windows is on simplifying things (tasks, interface, and everything else you can think of). You can search for something without having to jump through hoops to do it. The following sections describe four common methods of searching for content on your system using the Search charm.

### Performing an Apps search

Windows 8 places a lot of apps on your system, and you'll install even more. After a while, it becomes hard to remember whether you have a particular app installed and where

Windows installed it. An app search can make it a lot easier for you to find a particular app. The following steps tell you how to perform an app search:

1. **Press Win+C.**

   You see the Charms bar.

2. **Click Search.**

3. **Highlight the Apps option.**

   You see the Search panel, shown in Figure 1-15. Notice that a list of apps appears to the left of the panel. This list contains all registered apps on your system. You won't be able to find an executable file on your system that the Windows installer hasn't registered.

**Figure 1-15**

4. **Begin typing the name of the app you want to find.**

   The Search feature automatically begins reducing the size of the list as you type. Figure 1-16 shows a typical example of what happens when you type the letters *St*. Windows has found three possible apps that contain the letters *St* in their names.

**Figure 1-16**

5. **Click the app tile for the app you want to start.**

   Windows starts the app so that you can use it. You can also perform every other app-related task in this panel, such as pinning the app to the Start screen.

### Performing a Settings search

Past versions of Windows could sometimes make it hard to figure out how to change a setting. In fact, entire books discuss the topic of how to make settings changes with the least amount of difficulty. Even with the help these books provided, individual system differences sometimes made it difficult to figure out how to change a setting. Windows 8 partially corrects this problem by creating a Settings search feature that helps you locate the settings you need to change. The feature works only partially because it appears to help only with Windows 8 features and (possibly) certain Windows 8 apps. You can't use this feature to locate and change settings for your Desktop application. Even so, having this feature available means that you spend a lot less time trying to figure out how to change a setting. The following steps describe how to search for a setting you need to modify:

1. **Press Win+C.**

   You see the Charms bar.

2. **Click Search.**

3. **Highlight the Settings option.**

   You see a blank Search panel. Trying to show all the settings that Windows has to offer would be confusing, so you should expect to see nothing at this point.

4. **Type a term that reflects the setting you want to change.**

   The example in Figure 1-17 uses the word *account,* and you see all account-related settings. Notice that a list of account-related settings appears in the area to the left of the Search panel.

**Figure 1-17**

The icon next to a Settings tile tells you what sort of setting the tile represents. Figure 1-17 shows four commonly used Settings icons:

 • **Personal:** The gear-shaped icon always provides access to your personal settings.

 • **Group:** When you see an icon with two people in it, the associated setting affects a group, or multiple people. In most cases, you must have an administrator account to change a group setting.

 • **Action Center:** A number of settings, such as those used to control the User Account Control (UAC) and the network firewall, appear as part of the Action Center, which Windows always represents by an icon with a flag in it.

 • **System:** Some settings affect the entire system. For example, if you change the settings on your display, they affect the system as a whole with no regard for the user who's currently working with it. *Environment variables* (settings that control, for example, where Windows looks for applications — the *application path*) affect every application on the system, but you can change them for everyone who uses the computer or only for a specific user. System settings always appear with a monitor icon.

5. **Click the Settings tile for the setting you want to change.**

Windows displays the screen or dialog box for the setting you want to change. You see a number of these screens and dialog boxes in later parts of this book.

### Performing a Files search

Finding the files you need is hard at times, especially with people storing, in some cases, tens of thousands of data files on their systems. The Files search looks for files in either your personal or HomeGroup locations. It doesn't search for files just anywhere on the system. For example, if you tell the Files search to look for a data file on your network drive, it simply tells you that it can't find anything.

To use the HomeGroup locations, you must be part of a *HomeGroup* (a place where people with a common interest or as part of a common workgroup can share data) that has shared file resources. (The "Becoming Part of a Workgroup" section of Part 8 describes how to become part of a HomeGroup.) Otherwise, as when you look for files on a network drive, the File search doesn't find anything for you. With this in mind, the following steps describe how to use the Files search to locate one or more files in one of the locations that it can work with:

1. **Press Win+C.**

You see the Charms bar.

2. **Click Search.**

3. **Highlight the Files option.**

You see a blank Files panel. Windows needs some criteria on which to search for files:

- **\*.\*:** The most common criterion is to search for all files by using the \*.\* wildcard. The asterisk means "search for everything," and \*.\* means "search for every filename with every extension".

- **Specific file type:** Most applications produce one or more specific file types. For example, when you work with Word, you can create either .DOC (old style) or .DOCX (new style) files. If you tell Windows to search for \*.DOC, it locates every old-style Word document for you. Telling Windows to search for \*.DOC\* will return filenames with either the .DOC or the .DOCX file extension.

- **Files with specific letters:** As with any other search, you don't need to know anything about fancy file-names or file extensions to use Files search. If you type the word *welcome,* Windows locates every file with the word *welcome* anywhere in its name for you.

4. **(Optional) Select a search location, either Files or HomeGroup, by clicking the down arrow next to Files and choosing an option from the drop-down list box.**

   The default setting is to search your personal files. When you select HomeGroup, the heading changes from Files to HomeGroup.

5. **Type a criterion for your search in the Search field and click Search (the magnifying glass icon).**

   Windows displays the results of the search. Figure 1-18 shows typical results for the *.* wildcard search. Notice that the search displays all results by default. However, you can click specific folder results (Pictures and Other, in this case) to see only the results from that folder.

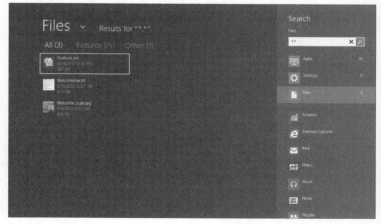

**Figure 1-18**

6. **Click the file tile for the file you want to open.**

   Windows automatically opens the file using its default application. Unlike other parts of Windows, right-clicking the file tile doesn't produce a list of alternatives for work-ing with the file, such as using an alternative application or printing it instead of opening it.

## Performing an app-specific search

Many Windows 8 apps can use the Search charm provided with Windows. (Desktop applications can't use the Search charm, for the most part.) For example, you might choose to look for specific news items. To perform a search for specific news, you click the News option in Search and type the keyword for the item you want to see. The following steps describe how to perform an app-specific search:

1. **Press Win+C.**

   You see the Charms bar.

2. **Click Search.**

3. **Highlight the option for the application you want to use.**

   Windows starts the application if you haven't already started it.

   Always wait for the application to start before you type a search term.

4. **After the application has started, type a search term in the search field and click Search (the magnifying glass icon).**

   Windows performs the search. Figure 1-19 shows some results of working with the News app.

**Figure 1-19**

5. **Click the link, tile, or picture of the item you want to see in detail, just as if you were using the app normally.**

Windows sends the request to the app, which displays the requested information in standard full-screen mode.

## Using the Share charm

The Share charm lets you share content with other people. To share content, you must first select an app. For example, you might see an app that you really like in the store and want to make a gift suggestion to someone. To share this content, you must have the gift selected and then display the sharing options by pressing Win+C and then choosing the Share charm. Figure 1-20 shows typical results for sharing something from the Store app.

**Figure 1-20**

The sharing options you see when working with the Share charm depend on the content provider. For example, when viewing a newspaper article, you may not see any sharing options. This is because the content provider has stipulated that the content is copyrighted. Windows 8 ensures that you respect any content protections placed on content by its originator.

The Share charm doesn't work with content from Desktop applications. To share something from a Desktop application, you must rely on the traditional sharing features that older versions of Windows provide. The following sections describe the methods that you can commonly use to share content with others.

### Sharing using e-mail

E-mail sharing relies on your Windows Live ID account, not any on other account you may normally use. For example, if you normally rely on using Outlook, the Share charm ignores it. You must have a Hotmail account, a Google account, or an Exchange account connected with the e-mail address you provide. You get a Hotmail account with your Windows Live ID by default. The following steps describe how to share content using e-mail:

*1.* **Open the app you want to work with and select the content you want to share.**

It's important that you see what you want to share onscreen before you attempt to share it.

*2.* **Press Win+C.**

You see the Charms bar.

*3.* **Click Share.**

You see the Share pane, which contains options for sharing the content you selected.

*4.* **Click Mail.**

Windows starts the Mail app, if it isn't already started. If you haven't already logged in to your Windows Live ID account, Windows displays the screen shown in Figure 1-21, where you can log in to it.

**Figure 1-21**

*5.* **(Optional) Log in to your Windows Live ID account.**

The Mail app connects to whatever account you have set up with Windows to work as e-mail. You see a screen similar to the one in Figure 1-22 for sharing the information with others.

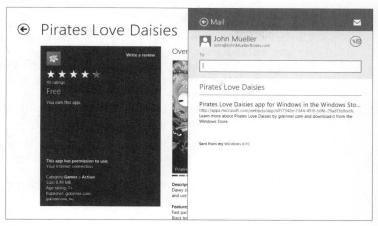

**Figure 1-22**

6.  **Type the name of the recipient in the To field provided and click Send E-Mail. (It's the icon in the upper-right corner; refer to Figure 1-22.)**

    Windows sends the e-mail to the person you requested.

### Sharing with a specific person

The Mail option works with all the various kinds of e-mail that you can connect with using Windows 8. The People option works with other kinds of people connections, such as Facebook, Twitter, and LinkedIn. To use this feature, you must first open the People app and create a connection to your account. Even though the People app lets you create connections to your e-mail accounts on Google, Hotmail, or Exchange Server, the accounts that matter for this option are the other connection types, such as Facebook. Once you have a connection created, you use the same steps for sharing content with your Facebook, Twitter, and LinkedIn accounts as you do for sharing by e-mail.

## Using the Start charm

The charm that you'll probably use most often is Start. Clicking the Start charm while on the Start screen takes you to the Desktop interface, where you can work with traditional Windows applications in an environment reminiscent of Windows 7. The Start charm is the only charm that has no options and never changes, depending on the app you're using.

## Using the Devices charm

The Devices charm displays a list of alternative devices on your system that can receive app content. For example, you might have a camera attached to your system and want to send content from the camera to a second display that's attached to the system. The device need not be a standard display — this feature also works for projectors and other devices you attach to your system that can receive output from an app.

As with many Windows 8 features, the Devices charm doesn't allow you to output content that's protected by the content originator. For example, you can't display a news story on a large screen using a projector when the wire service protects the content in some manner. In addition, this charm doesn't work with Desktop applications.

The number of devices you see in this charm depends on your system setup. You'll see, at a minimum, an option to work with a second monitor, even when you don't have a second monitor connected to your machine. The following steps describe how to send content to a second monitor:

1. **Press Win+C.**

   You see the Charms bar.

2. **Click Devices.**

   You see the Devices panel.

3. **Select the device you want to use.**

   Windows displays a list of device projection methods. The method list varies according to device and application. Figure 1-23 shows some typical examples of the choices you'll see.

4. **Choose a device projection method.**

   Windows projects content from the app using the projection device.

Figure 1-23

## Utilizing the Settings charm

The Settings charm changes constantly as you work with Windows 8. Every app, including the Start screen, has its own set of settings. Consequently, the content of this panel depends on the app you have in use at the time. To display the Settings charm, press Win+C and then choose Settings. Figure 1-24 shows a typical display of settings for the Calendar app.

Figure 1-24

The upper half of the panel contains settings specific to this app. For example, you can set the accounts associated with this app so that changes to the Calendar app also reflect in the associated account. The help associated with the app contains information about modifying these settings.

The lower half of the panel contains machine-specific settings that don't change. For example, when you click Power, you see options for shutting down your system, logging off, or placing the machine in Hibernate mode. In fact, the section "What You Can Do: Shutting Down Your System" in The Big Picture tells you how to work with this setting. The remainder of this book discusses some of these settings that you see every time you work with the Settings charm.

## Using Location Data

At times, an app needs to know your location in order to provide complete information. For example, the Maps app uses your location information to help you find the best way to get from your house to a friend's house. Whenever an app needs your location information, you see the screen grayed out and a question like the one shown in Figure 1-25.

**Figure 1-25**

The app never assumes that you've granted permission for all time. You see the request every time you start the app. If you give your permission to use the location information, the app automatically uses it to customize the content.

Of course, you can always choose not to allow the use of your location data. Many people avoid doing so because of privacy concerns. Apps such as Maps will still work just fine — the only difference is that you'll need to provide the location information manually.

# Part 2

# Navigating the Desktop Interface

Even if you eventually plan to use Windows 8 mainly with Windows 8 apps, the fact is that you'll commonly use Desktop applications at the outset because there won't be Windows 8 apps to meet every need. You'll find that you have to use Desktop applications for administration and other tasks until Microsoft creates Windows 8 app equivalents as well. In short, you won't get rid of the Desktop application interface anytime soon.

This part focuses on helping you work with the Desktop interface as efficiently as possible. Windows 8 really does have two separate interfaces, and you'll find that while the two interfaces can interact, you'll mainly spend time moving between the two for now. As shown in Part 1, many Start screen charms features don't even support Desktop applications, so you still need to use the same techniques as you used in the past to work with your Desktop applications.

## In this part . . .

- ✔ **Moving Between the Start Screen and Desktop**
- ✔ **Bringing Back the Start Menu**
- ✔ **Configuring the Desktop Icons**
- ✔ **Configuring the Taskbar**
- ✔ **Setting Up Jump Lists**
- ✔ **Setting Up Toolbars**

# *Moving Between the Start Screen and Desktop*

Some activities automatically cause a switch between the Start screen and Desktop interface. For example, when you open a Desktop application (such as Internet Explorer) using the Start screen, Windows 8 automatically transfers control to the Desktop interface so that you can see the copy of Internet Explorer start. However, many other activities require that you switch between the Start screen and Desktop interface manually. The following sections provide quick methods you can use to display each interface.

## Displaying the Desktop interface

You have a number of choices for displaying the Desktop interface from the Start screen. Of course, opening a Desktop application is one way. The easiest method of opening the Desktop interface is to click the Desktop tile on the Start screen. You can also use these other techniques for displaying the Desktop interface:

- ✔ Press the Windows key to toggle between the Start screen and the last application used.

- ✔ Press Win+C and then click Start on the Charms bar, as shown in Figure 2-1.

- ✔ Press Win+Tab to cycle between open applications (pressing Win+Shift+Tab cycles between them in reverse), as shown in Figure 2-2.

## Displaying the Start screen

Once you're in the Desktop interface, you'll eventually need to go back to the Start screen. Some of the same techniques that work to move you to the Desktop interface also move you back to the Start screen. However, the easiest way to access the Start screen from the Desktop interface is to move the mouse cursor to the lower-left corner of the screen. The Start screen icon appears, as shown in Figure 2-3.

**Figure 2-1**

**Figure 2-2**

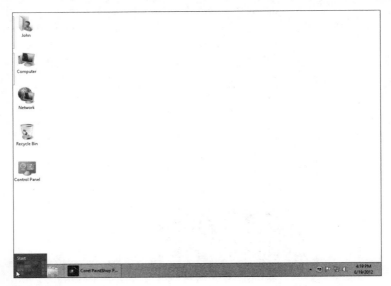

**Figure 2-3**

Click the Start screen icon to move to the Start screen. You can also use these options:

- Press the Windows key to display the Start screen. (Pressing the Windows key again displays the last application you used in the Desktop interface.)

- Press Win+C and then click Start on the Charms bar. (Performing this task a second time takes you to the last application you used in the Desktop interface.)

- Press Win+Shift+Tab to cycle between open applications. (The Start screen always appears as the last item on this list.)

# *Bringing Back the Start Menu*

A lot of people have complained about losing the Start menu in Windows 8. Microsoft is equally determined to make the Start menu missing in action. Fortunately, a third party, LeeSoft, has stepped in to provide an alternative, named ViStart. Originally, this product was designed to provide a Vista-style Start menu for Windows XP users. However, the vendor has constantly updated ViStart, and it works great in Windows 8 to provide a replacement for the missing Start menu.

## Downloading the ViStart replacement

Before you can do anything, you need a copy of ViStart. Follow these steps to get started:

1. **Go to** `www.lee-soft.com/vistart` **and click the Download button in the center of the page.**

   Internet Explorer asks whether you want to run or save the file named `windows-start-menu-vistart.exe`. You may see a warning that the file could harm your computer when you try to download it. The ViStart application is perfectly safe to download from this location.

2. **Click Save.**

   Internet Explorer begins downloading the file. Note where Internet Explorer saves the file. (Normally, it's the `C:\Users\<UserName>\Downloads` folder on your system.) Saving the file makes it easier to uninstall ViStart later if you decide that you don't want it. At some point, Internet Explorer indicates that the download has completed.

3. **Click Open Folder.**

   Internet Explorer displays the download folder, which has the `windows-start-menu-vistart.exe` file in it.

## Installing ViStart

After you have a copy of the executable file (see the previous section), you can install it on your system. Normally, you can simply follow the prompts. However, ViStart includes a wealth of extras that you probably don't want installed on your system. The following procedure helps you install ViStart without these extras:

1. **Double-click** `windows-start-menu-vistart.exe` **in the download folder that I tell you how to open in the preceding section.**

   You see the User Account Control dialog box, asking whether you trust ViStart to make changes to the system.

2. **Click Yes.**

   After a few moments, you see the ViStart Setup Wizard Welcome screen.

3. **Click Next.**

   The wizard presents the licensing terms for ViStart. Make sure to read these terms thoroughly to ensure that you understand them.

4. **Click Accept (when you agree with the terms).**

   You momentarily see a dialog box appear, and then a second InstallManager Setup dialog box, like the one in Figure 2-4, appears. This second dialog box asks whether you want to install the product described on the screen. Unless you want to install the Babylon products that are listed, click Decline.

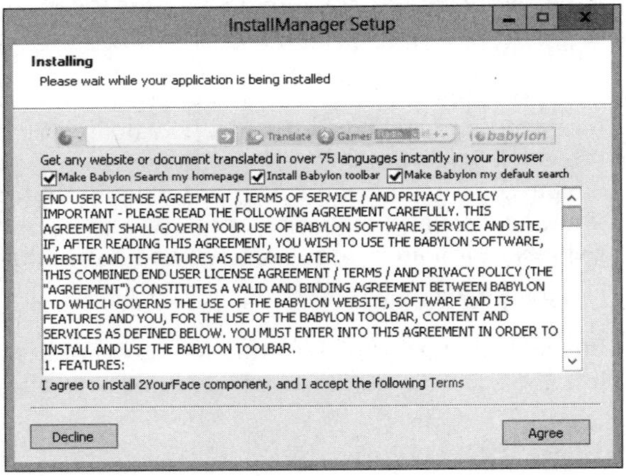

**Figure 2-4**

5. **Click Decline to avoid installing the Babylon products.**

   You see another page (see Figure 2-5) asking whether you want to install support for WeCare.com. When you prefer not to support this group, click Decline.

6. **Click Decline to avoid installing the WeCare product.**

   The wizard completes the installation. You see a new tab opened in Internet Explorer, leading to the LeeSoft site at `www.lee-soft.com/vistart/thankyou.html`, which thanks you for installing ViStart. You also see a small message box telling you that ViStart is loading. ViStart is ready for use.

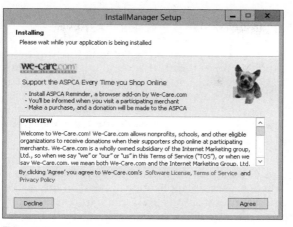

**Figure 2-5**

# Using ViStart

At this point, you'll notice that the Start icon appears in the lower-left corner of the display on the Taskbar, just as it appears in older versions of Windows. Click this icon and you see the standard Start menu, as shown in Figure 2-6.

**Figure 2-6**

ViStart makes a few changes to the way Windows 8 works. For example, you'll find that pressing the Windows key displays the Start menu now rather than taking you to the Start screen. You can still display the Start screen icon in the lower-left corner of the display to go to the Start screen. In addition, the Charms bar is still accessible, so you can press Win+C and then click Start to see the Start screen. Likewise, you can press Win+Tab to cycle through the list of open applications, including Windows 8 apps. The only real difference is that one shortcut no longer works as it did.

The Start menu contains most of the options it contains in earlier versions of Windows. Anything that's installed on your system in the form of a Desktop application appears in the list. For example, Figure 2-7 shows what my Start menu looks like when I click All Programs after installing a few Desktop applications.

**Figure 2-7**

Windows is missing a few items from previous versions. One of the first items that you notice is gone is any reference to the Desktop games (such as Solitaire) that Windows supported in the past. Before you get the idea to simply install a copy from an earlier version, you should know that the application will display a compatibility error message and refuse to work. Some options you can add back in. For example, you'll notice that the Command Prompt entry is missing. The "Adding a command prompt entry to the Start menu" section of Part 9 tells you how to add this feature back to the Start menu.

ViStart doesn't quite provide all the functionality of the old Start menu. Right-clicking an item in the Start menu does display a context menu in the latest version of the product, but the context menu is missing some options, such as the ability to set application properties. Unfortunately, you can't easily overcome these problems, but LeeSoft keeps making updates, so you may see this feature in the future.

## Modifying the ViStart options

You need to know about one necessary ViStart feature — changing the options. Open the Start menu and click the arrow next to *Shut Down* to display the context menu shown in Figure 2-8.

**Figure 2-8**

Click Options. You see the Options dialog box shown in Figure 2-9.

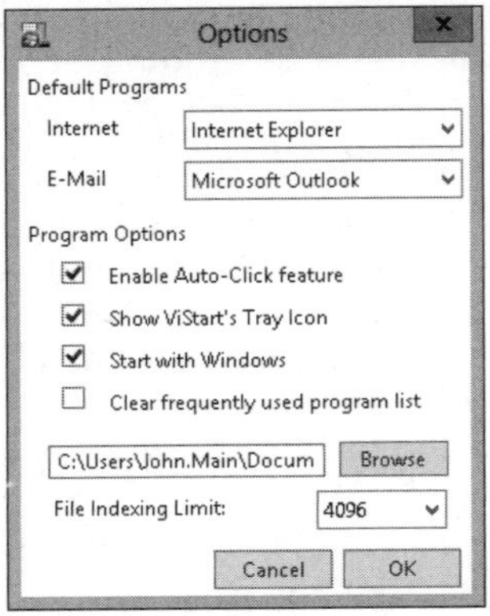

**Figure 2-9**

This dialog box lets you choose basic Desktop environment options, such as browser and e-mail application. You can also customize how ViStart works. However, in most cases, you don't have to change any of these ViStart-specific options because Windows 8 contains no standard Start menu alternative. Here's a quick overview of the ViStart options:

- ✓ **Enable Auto-Click Feature:** Tells ViStart to mimic the auto-click feature from Vista. When you hover the mouse cursor over an item that has the autoclick feature enabled, the feature is automatically clicked after a second or two.

- ✓ **Show ViStart's Tray Icon:** Displays the ViStart icon in the Notification Area. This addition lets you perform tasks, such as shutting down the system, by right-clicking the Notification Area icon instead of using the Start menu.

- ✓ **Start with Windows:** Tells ViStart to start automatically when you start Windows. Keep this option checked.

- ✓ **Clear Frequently Used Program List:** When checked, automatically clears the list of frequently used applications every time the user signs out. This safety feature is good for publicly used machines, but it can make it harder to use ViStart on your personal machine because the Start menu doesn't track the applications you use most often.

- ✓ **File location field:** Determines the location of the user's personal data. Click Browse to display a dialog box that lets you graphically select the file location.

- ✓ **File Indexing Limit:** Defines the maximum number of files that ViStart will index.

# Configuring the Desktop Icons

The Desktop takes on added meaning in Windows 8 because Microsoft has made it harder to use features that you may have relied on in older versions. The Windows Desktop, like your physical desktop, is a good place to put items you want to work with. Of course, when the Desktop becomes too cluttered with icons, it behaves much like your physical desktop in *hiding* the work you need to do. Therefore, it's a good idea to keep your Desktop clean.

Icons come in two forms: Windows-specific and user-specific. The "Placing applications on the Desktop" section of The Big Picture explains how to add and remove Windows-specific applications from your Desktop. The icons provide access to Windows features such as the Recycle Bin.

The following sections describe how to add user-specific icons to the Desktop and remove them when they're no longer needed. A user-specific icon is normally a shortcut to an application, folder, or file, but can be a shortcut to anything you want. For that matter, you can create original folders to hold items you need.

## Adding icons to the Desktop

The best way to organize your Desktop is to provide access to the content you need rather than to a list of applications. Windows creates associations between files and applications for you. When you double-click a Word file, Windows automatically opens Word for you. However, when you choose not to use Word for that file, you can right-click the file and choose WordPad instead. Likewise, graphics files often have two or more useful applications associated with them on your system. Focusing on content lets you work in a way that's natural for most people. In general, people are concerned with content, not with applications.

To keep your Desktop neat, organize related content in folders, just as you would on your real desktop. When you need to work on a particular project, open that project folder and double-click the file you want to see. In most cases, the folder you use is the one holding the content on a local or network drive, but you can create your own folders for holding items by right-clicking the Desktop and choosing New⇨Folder from the context menu. You can type any name you want for the folder and press Enter to finish creating it.

Using shortcuts lets you keep the content in its original place and allows other people to access it. To create a shortcut to an application, a file, or a folder on your Desktop, right-click the original item and choose Copy from the context menu. Right-click the Desktop and choose Paste Shortcut from the context menu.

The shortcut appears wherever you paste it. When you want to see the shortcut in a folder, right-click the folder and choose Paste Shortcut from the context menu. You can also create multiple shortcuts. For example, two projects may require the same file. Simply create two shortcuts, one for each project, in their respective folders. The shortcut consumes very little disk space, and you won't replicate the file — both shortcuts point to the same file, so changes in one automatically reflect in the other.

## Organizing the icons

Whatever form of icon you provide on the Desktop, it's important to display them in a manner that makes their efficient use possible. Accomplishing this task means organizing the icons for easier access. You can manually move icons from one location to another, but most people will find it easier to rely on the automated organizational features in Windows 8.

The first choice you should make is how to display the icons. To make this selection, right-click the Desktop and select an option on the View menu, as shown in Figure 2-10.

| View ▶ | Large icons |
|---|---|
| Sort by ▶ | ● Medium icons |
| Refresh | Small icons |
| Paste | Auto arrange icons |
| Paste shortcut | ✓ Align icons to grid |
| Shared Folder Synchronization ▶ | ✓ Show desktop icons |
| New ▶ | ✓ Show desktop gadgets |
| Screen resolution | |
| Gadgets | |
| Personalize | |

**Figure 2-10**

You can use these features to your benefit when working on the Desktop. The following list describes these options and tells how you can use them to your benefit:

✔ **Large Icons, Medium Icons, Small Icons:** Defines the icon size. Use small icons to make it possible to display additional content items onscreen. Large icons help you see content detail when working with graphics.

✔ **Auto Arrange Icons:** Automatically rearranges new icons as you add them to the Desktop to match whatever criterion you provide.

✔ **Align Icons to Grid:** Automatically aligns the icons to provide an organized appearance. Clear this option when you want additional flexibility in arranging icons in a specific manner.

✔ **Show Desktop Icons:** Displays the icons you select. Clear this option to remove icons from the Desktop temporarily when you want to see something on the background or have space to work with additional gadgets.

✔ **Show Desktop Gadgets:** Displays the gadgets you select. Clear this option to remove gadgets from the Desktop temporarily, especially when you don't normally use gadgets to perform your work. In some cases, it may simply be easier to stop using gadgets completely if you find that they interfere with your work.

As mentioned, you can manually place icons in a specific order on the Desktop. Make sure you clear the Auto Arrange Icons option before you do so, however, to ensure that Windows doesn't change the order you're trying to create. Most people find that simply sorting the icons is all they need to do to use them easily. To sort items, right-click the Desktop and choose an option from the Sort By submenu, shown in Figure 2-11.

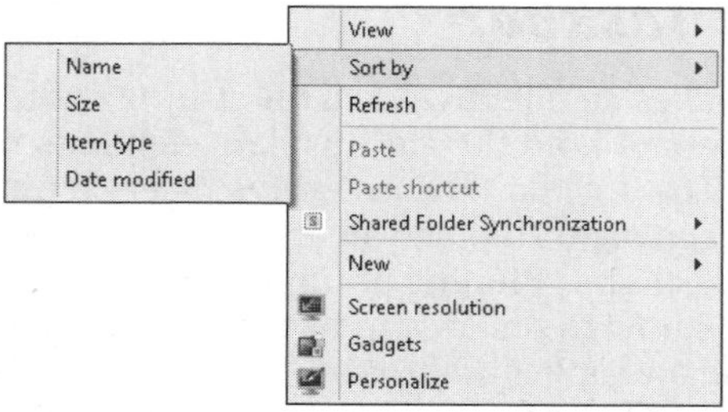

**Figure 2-11**

Unfortunately, you can't combine sort orders to obtain specific effects, such as separating files first by type and then by last modification date. (For whatever reason, Window has never checked the sort order that's in effect, as it does when you work with File Explorer.) The following list describes these sort options:

✔ **Name:** Sorts icons by name. This is an especially effective way to work with folders because the project names appear in essentially the same order as they would in a filing cabinet.

The sorting options are reversible so that you can sort items in either ascending or descending order. For example, if the folders are sorted in ascending name order, selecting Name again sorts them in descending name order.

✔ **Size:** Sorts icons by size. You normally use this option with files so that you can easily see the files based on the amount of content they provide.

✔ **Item Type:** Sorts icons by the kind of content each one contains. For example, you can use this option to place folders, files, and executables in separate sections. In addition, graphics files appear separately from word processing content.

✔ **Date Modified:** Sorts icons by the last time you modified them. Newer files appear either first or last in the list, depending on whether you select ascending or descending order. This option is especially effective when you tend to work on the most current files regularly.

## Configuring the Taskbar

The Desktop makes an effective area for storing content. You can create folders to hold the various data elements required for your work. The Taskbar is an effective place to put applications you use regularly. To place an application on the Taskbar, you pin it in place. The "Pinning or unpinning an app" section of Part 1 describes how to pin an app to the Start screen. The process for pinning an application to the Taskbar is similar, except that you can pin only Desktop applications. Use these steps to pin an application to the Taskbar:

*1.* **Press Win+C, and then click Start on the Charms bar.**

You see the Start screen.

2. **Press Win+Z or right-click the Start screen.**

   You see the Apps bar.

3. **Click All Apps.**

   You see the Apps screen.

4. **Right-click the Desktop application that you want to pin to the Taskbar.**

   You see the App bar showing the options for that application. Figure 2-12 shows what the App bar looks like for Word. Notice that Word provides the Pin to Taskbar option. Windows 8 apps don't provide this option.

**Figure 2-12**

5. **Click the Pin to Taskbar icon.**

   Windows adds the application to the Taskbar.

In addition to adding applications to the Taskbar, you can configure the Taskbar to behave in specific ways. Right-click the Taskbar and choose Properties from the context menu to display the Taskbar Properties dialog box, shown in Figure 2-13.

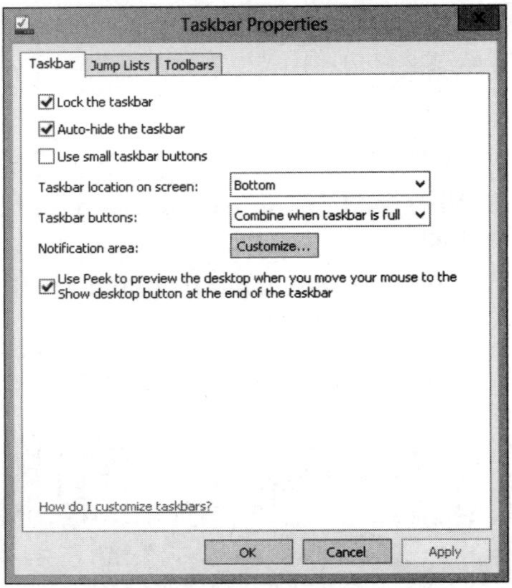

**Taskbar Properties**

Taskbar | Jump Lists | Toolbars

☑ Lock the taskbar
☑ Auto-hide the taskbar
☐ Use small taskbar buttons

Taskbar location on screen:      Bottom ▾

Taskbar buttons:                 Combine when taskbar is full ▾

Notification area:               Customize...

☑ Use Peek to preview the desktop when you move your mouse to the Show desktop button at the end of the taskbar

How do I customize taskbars?

OK    Cancel    Apply

**Figure 2-13**

These properties are similar to those found in older versions of Windows. The following list provides information on how to use each property:

- ✓ **Lock the Taskbar:** Prevents you from moving items on the Taskbar. This option helps preserve the setup you create.

- ✓ **Auto-hide the Taskbar:** Minimizes the Taskbar so that you can't see it while performing tasks. This option makes more space available for working with applications. Move the mouse cursor to the bottom of the display to show the Taskbar when needed.

- ✓ **Use Small Taskbar Buttons:** Reduces the size of the buttons used on the Taskbar, which allows you to display more buttons in the same space. However, using this option can make the buttons a tad hard to see.

- ✓ **Taskbar Location on Screen:** Determines whether the Taskbar appears on the top or bottom or the left or right side of your display. The default position is the bottom.

  When working with Windows 8, it's a bad idea to place the Taskbar on the right or left side of the display because Windows 8 uses those areas to display features such as the Charms bar.

✔ **Taskbar Buttons:** When you open multiple files using the same application, the Taskbar normally displays each file as a separate button. However, you can tell the Taskbar to combine these files into a single button when the Taskbar gets full or always to combine them to save space.

✔ **Notification Area:** Displays the Notification Area Icons dialog box, which allows you change how icons appear in the Notification Area. This feature works precisely the same as it did in previous versions of Windows.

✔ **Use Peek to Preview the Desktop:** Temporarily minimizes all applications so that you can see the Desktop. To use this feature, you move the mouse cursor to the right end of the Taskbar and hold it there. The Desktop appears as long as you keep the mouse cursor on the right side.

## Setting Up Jump Lists

A *Jump List* makes it possible to open a file by right-clicking its application's icon and choosing the file from the list that appears. Figure 2-14 shows an example of a Jump List for Word.

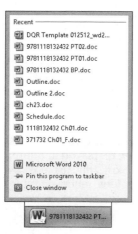

**Figure 2-14**

The list of files appears at the top of the Jump List. Three entries at the bottom of the Jump List provide access to the application itself, a means to pin the application to the Taskbar, and a way to close the current window.

Windows 8 provides additional settings for Jump Lists so that you can better control how they work. To modify these settings, right-click the Taskbar and choose Properties from the context menu to display the Taskbar Properties. Select the Jump Lists tab, shown in Figure 2-15.

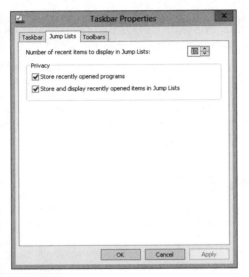

**Figure 2-15**

You have access to one setting that controls the Jump List and two settings that affect your privacy. Always clear the privacy settings on a public machine so that no one can walk behind you and see what you've done. The following list describes each of these settings:

- **Number of Recent Items to Display in Jump Lists:** Controls the number of items you see displayed in a Jump List. The default setting of ten items works fine for most people. When you open a large number of files, increasing this value can keep needed files on the Jump List longer. However, the longer you make the list, the more time you spend scanning it to look for the file. At some point, the Jump List loses its effectiveness as an aid for working with content faster.

✔ **Store Recently Opened Programs:** Stores a list of recently opened programs. Certain applications, such as File Explorer, display frequent places you visit and applications you use (rather than filenames). Clearing this option makes these programs no longer track this sort of information for you.

✔ **Store and Display Recently Opened Items in Jump Lists:** Stores a list of recently opened files. Many applications store filenames so that you can open them quickly the next time. Clearing this option means that you can't use Jump Lists to open files.

# Setting Up Toolbars

The Taskbar can provide access to multiple toolbars. A toolbar provides added access to a Windows element, such as the Desktop, or to a programmed element, such as a search engine. You can also create custom toolbars containing only the information you want. By default, Windows 8 provides access to the four toolbars listed in Figure 2-16.

In addition, a third party can create a custom toolbar and install it for you. Not every toolbar will work with Windows 8, so you need to experiment a little to find those that do. The following list describes the four default toolbars you can use:

✔ **Address:** Displays an address bar where you can type any location you want to see. Windows 8 provides the necessary functionality to make the connection work. For example, when you type a URL, you see a copy of Internet Explorer open to that location. Likewise, type the Universal Naming Convention (UNC) address of a location on your network drive, and Windows opens a copy of File Explorer so that you can see it.

✔ **Links:** Displays a list of favorites that you've stored on your machine. These links provide a quick means of opening online resources without starting a browser first.

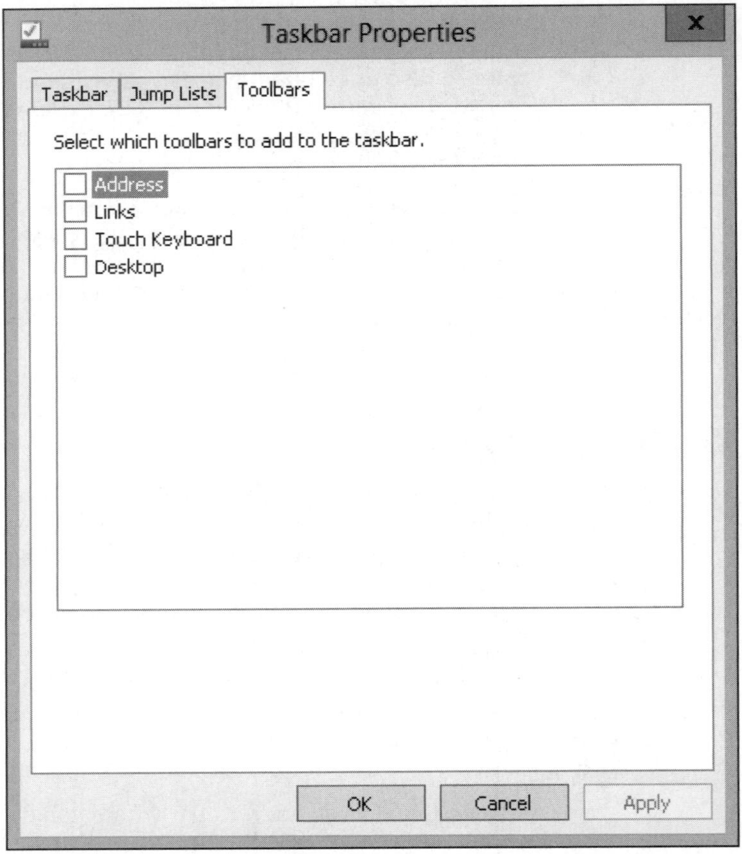

**Figure 2-16**

- ✔ **Touch Keyboard:** Shows a keyboard icon. Click the icon and you start the Touch Keyboard application that is used to type input when you have a touch screen capable device. The application opens a keyboard onscreen that you can use to type information.

- ✔ **Desktop:** Provides access to all items on your Desktop so that you can perform tasks (such as opening a folder to access a file you need) without first minimizing the applications you have running. Using this technique makes accessing Desktop icons quite speedy.

# Using the Standard Applications

Applications form the basis of interacting with a computer, but it's the *content* the applications manage that is the focus for most users. Windows 8 comes with a number of applications, and you can install your own applications as needed. Each of these applications helps a user manage content in some way. As stated in Part 1, Microsoft has set up new conditions for Windows 8 apps, but your Desktop applications will work the same as they did in previous versions of Windows. This part helps you clear a few hurdles when working with Desktop applications in Windows 8. When you complete this part, you'll be able to install, access, configure, manage, and uninstall Desktop applications as needed.

## In this part . . .

- Finding Your Applications
- Installing Applications
- Turning Windows Features On or Off
- Pinning Common Applications to the Taskbar
- Setting Up Applications to Run Under Windows 8
- Uninstalling Applications

# Finding Your Applications

When you install an application by using an installer, it normally registers the application with Windows. You see the application listed in the Programs and Features applet of the Control Panel. Use these steps to open the Programs and Features applet:

1.  **Press Win+C.**

    You see the Charms bar.

2.  **Click the Settings charm.**

    You see the Settings page.

3.  **Click Control Panel.**

    You see the Control Panel window.

4.  **Click the Programs group.**

    You see the Programs window.

5.  **Click the Programs and Features group.**

    You see the Programs and Features applet shown in Figure 3-1.

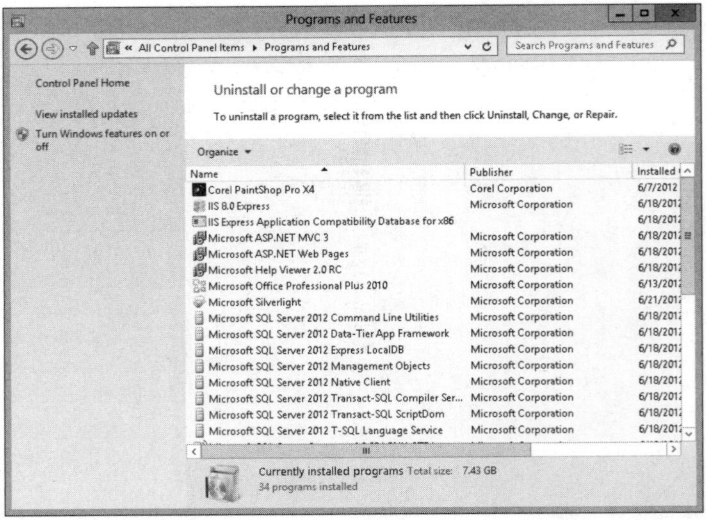

**Figure 3-1**

In addition, you can normally see the application listed on the Apps screen that you access by right-clicking the Start screen and then clicking All Apps. Figure 3-2 shows an example of the kinds of Desktop applications you'll see.

**Figure 3-2**

However, sometimes an application installs properly and appears in the Programs and Features list but still doesn't appear on the Apps screen. For that matter, there are times when you install a simple application by downloading and unarchiving it to a specific folder on your machine, in which case the executable file (the application) doesn't appear in the Programs and Features list or on the Apps screen. You have a number of options you can exercise when this situation occurs, as described in the following list:

- Press Win+R to display the Run dialog box, and then type the application's name to start it. If the application doesn't run, try locating it by clicking Browse in the Run dialog box.

- Open a copy of File Explorer, locate the application on disk, and then double-click it to start it.

- Open a command prompt and use this procedure to locate the executable:

  1. **Press Win.**

Windows displays the Start screen.

2. **Right-click the Start screen and choose All Apps from the App bar.**

   You see the Apps screen.

3. **Click Command Prompt in the Windows System group.**

   Windows creates a command prompt for you.

4. **Type** CD \ **and press Enter.**

   The prompt changes to show the root directory on the current drive.

5. **Type** Dir *<Executable Name>* /s **and press Enter.**

   Windows searches the hard drive for the executable you need and displays its location. For example, if you search for WinWord.exe (the Word executable), you find that it's located at C:\Program Files\Microsoft Office\Office14 when working with Word 2010.

6. **Locate the directory using File Explorer and double-click the executable file.**

   Windows starts the application for you.

You can pin any running application to the Taskbar. The "Using a running application" section, later in this part, describes how to perform this task. Pinning hard-to-locate applications that you use often saves considerable time in the end.

# Installing Applications

Software providers now employ a number of techniques when distributing software. It's possible to simply send the executable file in an e-mail, save the executable to disk, and then run the application immediately. Some applications aren't even stored on your machine; they run on a remote server instead (requiring only configuration, not installation). You see the application presented on your machine through a browser or another interface. In fact, you could probably write an entire book on the art of installing software on a PC. However, most software distribution follows one of three routes:

✔ CD or DVD

- Downloaded file
- Installer that accesses the installation files on a remote server

This book doesn't provide comprehensive coverage of every installation technique. However, it covers the three common techniques in the sections that follow.

## Using a CD or DVD

In times past, you could simply place a CD or DVD in a removable drive and the installer would run. This technique proved dangerous, however, because the installer could do anything during the first few moments of the installation routine and the user would never know. Consequently, Windows 8 now displays a *toast* (a special sort of message box containing a notification in this case) asking how you want to work with a CD or DVD like the one shown in Figure 3-3.

DVD RW Drive (E:) H3_SHADOW
Tap to choose what happens with this disc.

**Figure 3-3**

The toast displays for only a few seconds and then fades away without doing anything unless you click it. When you click the toast, you see a number of options for dealing with the CD or DVD, like the ones shown in Figure 3-4.

DVD RW Drive (E:) H3_SHA...

Choose what to do with this disc.

**Install or run program from your media**

Run AUTORUN.EXE
Publisher not specified

**Other choices**

Open folder to view files
Windows Explorer

Take no action

**Figure 3-4**

Only when you click the Run AUTORUN.EXE option does the automatic installer start to perform its task. Otherwise, the CD or DVD simply waits for you to start the installer manually. Click Open Folder to View Files to start a copy of File Explorer that opens to the drive containing the removable media. At this point, you can double-click Setup.exe (or another file) to start the installation.

Even though Windows 8 does a good job of making the AutoRun feature ineffective, a user can still automatically start an installation. With this in mind, some organizations simply disable AutoRun so that the user can never start an installation automatically. You can find instructions for performing this task at www.addictivetips.com/windows-tips/disable-autorun-autoplay-in-windows-7.

## Using a downloaded file

Many sites provide files you can download. These files contain executable code for an application you want to run. Downloaded files include those you receive from locations other than a browser. For example, someone can send you an executable in your e-mail. No matter what the source of the download file is, the file contains executable code that you must work with in some way to install the application.

Some executable code comes in compact form. A script or another small, executable file (perhaps a self-contained .EXE file) can provide limited functionality to perform a specific task. The file can appear in an archive, such as a .ZIP file, but the result is the same. To use this sort of executable, you simply place it in a folder on your system and double-click the file. The application appears on neither the Programs and Features list nor the Apps screen, but it's still perfectly usable.

Other downloaded applications have multiple files. They might be packed in an archive or appear in a special installer executable. Depending on how the developer designed the application, unarchiving (as needed) and double-clicking the installer installs the application on your machine. In this case, the application definitely appears in the Programs and Files list, but still might not appear on the Apps screen.

Nefarious individuals sometimes try to trick you into downloading what looks like a perfectly good application that hides viruses galore. As with any application, you need to know the source of the application you download to install. Always download applications from sites you know and vendors you trust. Accept e-mails only from individuals you know and trust. It's usually a good idea to verify that the e-mail came from that individual before you install the application attached to it.

## Running from a remote location

Many applications install from remote locations. In some cases, you download a small, local, installer executable to your hard drive, but in other cases you simply click a link to start the installation. The use of a remote location lets the developer upgrade the application and ensures that you always get the most recent version. In addition, using a remote location makes it possible to control distribution of the application with greater ease and lets the developer obtain more information about your system for a custom install. All Windows 8 apps work this way, and many Desktop applications work this way as well.

 Of the methods for installing an application, using a remote location poses the most significant threat to the installing machine because you can't easily verify that the application is uncorrupted. Someone can easily steal the URL for a remote location and redirect you to a site containing a compromised file. It's also possible for the file on the remote location to become compromised. Some vendors provide methods for you to verify the file before you install it. Always follow the vendor's advice and verify the file, even if you trust the site you used for the download.

# Turning Windows Features On or Off

As with many previous versions of Windows, Windows 8 provides separate support for Windows features. You turn a Windows feature on or off — making it accessible or inaccessible to users on the system. The Windows 8 feature doesn't actually install or uninstall. The following procedure shows how to turn Windows 8 features on or off as needed:

*1.* **Press Win+C.**

You see the Charms bar.

*2.* **Click the Settings charm.**

You see the Settings page.

*3.* **Click Control Panel.**

You see the Control Panel window, as shown in Figure 3-5.

**Figure 3-5**

4. **Click Programs.**

   Windows displays a list of actions you can perform with programs. (See Figure 3-6.) Only administrators or those you can elevate privileges to have access to the Turn Windows Features On or Off link, as indicated by the shield icon. Whenever you see the shield icon next to a link in the Control Panel, you know that you need additional privileges to use that feature.

**Figure 3-6**

5. **Click Turn Windows Features On or Off.**

Windows displays a list of features, as shown in Figure 3-7. Empty check boxes represent applications that are turned off. Check boxes containing a check represent applications that are completely on (fully installed). When you see a square within a check box, the entry is part of a complex application that you've partially turned on (some features are accessible, but others aren't).

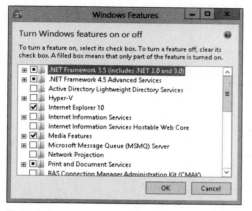

**Figure 3-7**

*6.* **Make any required changes to the entries in the Windows Features dialog box and click OK.**

Windows makes the required features accessible or inaccessible as needed.

# Pinning Common Applications to the Taskbar

Earlier parts of this book provide a brief overview of pinning applications. For example, the "Configuring the Taskbar" section of Part 2 describes how to pin to the Taskbar a Desktop application found on the Start screen.

It's important to understand that pinning an application is an efficiency step, when you work with an application often enough that you must have it immediately accessible. If you aren't using an application regularly, don't pin it, because you'll simply clutter the interface. (Microsoft is trying to avoid clutter in Windows 8 at all costs.) The following sections describe three methods for pinning an application.

## Using a running application

Whenever you run an application, Windows 8 provides a Jump List with it. The top of the Jump List contains the names of files you've opened or locations you've visited using that application. At the bottom of the Jump List, you find an entry for pinning the application. (See Figure 3-8.)

**Figure 3-8**

When you click Pin this Program to the Taskbar, the application is pinned until you unpin it. Pinning using this approach is as effective as any other technique you might use. The result is that the application is available at all times until you unpin it.

## Using File Explorer

You can also pin any application you find in File Explorer to the Start screen or the Taskbar. Right-click the application and you see the required options on the context menu, as shown in Figure 3-9.

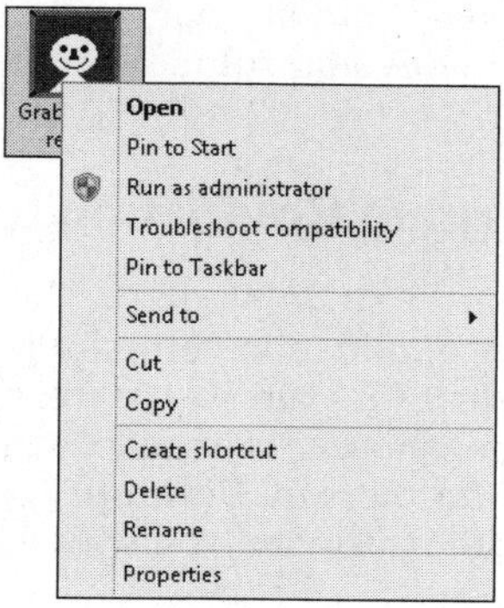

**Figure 3-9**

To pin the application to the Start screen, choose Pin to Start. Likewise, when you want to pin the application to the Taskbar, choose Pin to Taskbar. The pin options will change to unpin options when you pin an application to either the Start screen or the Taskbar. Choose Unpin from Start or Unpin from Taskbar to unpin an application that you no longer want pinned to these locations.

# Setting Up Applications to Run Under Windows 8

Many applications need help to run under Windows 8 — even applications that ran fine under Windows 7. As with all previous versions of Windows, Microsoft has tweaked Windows 8 in ways that can prevent applications from running correctly (or at all).

Before you do anything else, try the application to determine whether it will work with changes to settings. In addition, check the vendor site to determine whether the vendor has a custom fix for the problem. The best you can hope to achieve in Windows 8 is to locate a quick fix for any compatibility issues your application may present. It's always better to get a solution specifically designed for that application, when available.

The following sections describe techniques you can use to overcome application compatibility problems quickly. Of course, Microsoft continually improves the ability of Windows 8 to overcome compatibility issues, but some applications may never run. When testing compatibility for a larger organization, make sure you have backup plans and alternative applications in mind to ensure that you can develop solutions for compatibility issues.

## Making use of the Program Compatibility Troubleshooter

The easiest method of solving application compatibility problems is to tell Windows 8 to do it for you. Fortunately, the Program Compatibility Troubleshooter is available throughout Windows 8 — including the Start screen, Desktop, Taskbar, and File Explorer. The following steps provide you with a guide on how to perform this task:

*1.* **Right-click the application icon and choose Troubleshoot Compatibility from the context menu.**

The Program Compatibility Troubleshooter starts, analyzes potential problems with your application, and formulates a response. It then presents a list of choices for resolving the compatibility issue, like the one shown in Figure 3-10.

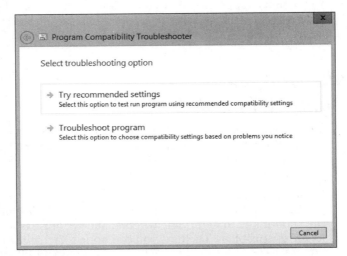

**Figure 3-10**

2. **Click the Try Recommended Settings option.**

The Program Compatibility Troubleshooter applies the settings to the application and then displays a dialog box asking you to test the application to determine whether the settings work.

**3. Click Test the Application.**

Windows attempts to start the application. When the settings are correct, the application starts as normal with as much functionality as it can provide.

**4. Exit the application.**

You see the Program Compatibility Troubleshooter dialog box again.

**5. Click Next.**

The Program Compatibility Troubleshooter presents three options that represent the possible outcomes, as shown in Figure 3-11.

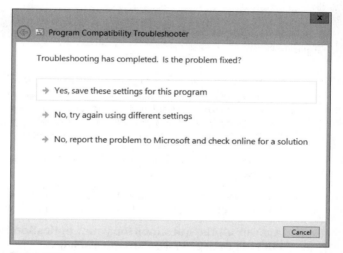

Figure 3-11

**6. Click the appropriate choice.**

Take one of these three paths, depending on your choice:

- When you click Yes, Save These Settings for This Program, you're finished. Click Close to close the Windows Compatibility Troubleshooter. The application will run just as it did when you tested it.

- When you click No, Try Again Using Different Settings, the Program Compatibility Troubleshooter asks you a number of questions about application behavior, as shown in Figure 3-12. Proceed to Step 7.

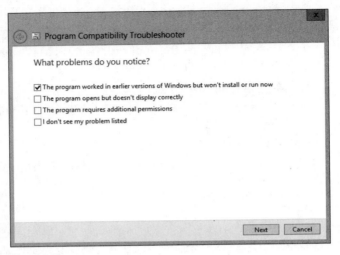

**Figure 3-12**

- When you click No, Report the Problem to Microsoft and Check Online for a Solution, the Program Compatibility Troubleshooter creates a report for Microsoft and then displays a Troubleshooting Has Completed dialog box. Proceed to Step 9.

7. **Select the options that match your application's behavior and then click Next.**

   The Program Compatibility Troubleshooter asks for specific behavior information, as shown in Figure 3-13.

8. **Answer all the questions for your application in turn, clicking Next after you answer each one.**

   Eventually, the Program Compatibility Troubleshooter asks you to test the application. Proceed to Step 3.

9. **Click Close the Troubleshooter.**

   At this point, the best option is to try to configure the application manually.

## Modifying the configuration manually

Sometimes, the automation for fixing a problem in your application just doesn't work. No matter how many times you run the Program Compatibility Troubleshooter, it comes up with a solution that doesn't work. In this case, you can try to manually

configure the compatibility options for the application. To
perform this task, right-click the application icon and choose
Properties from the context menu. Select the Compatibility tab
and you see the compatibility options shown in Figure 3-14.

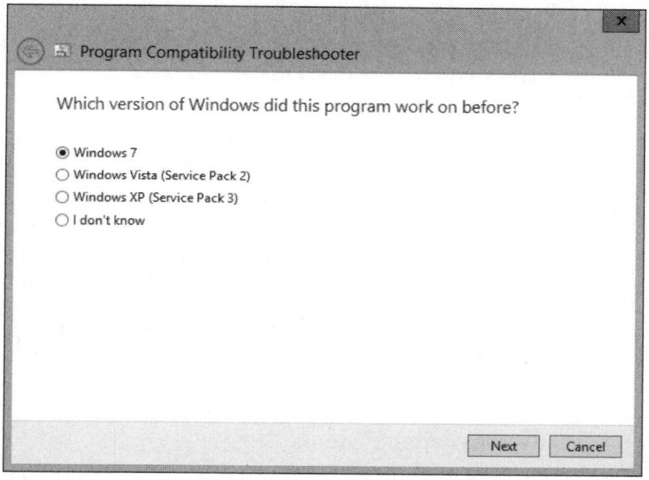

**Figure 3-13**

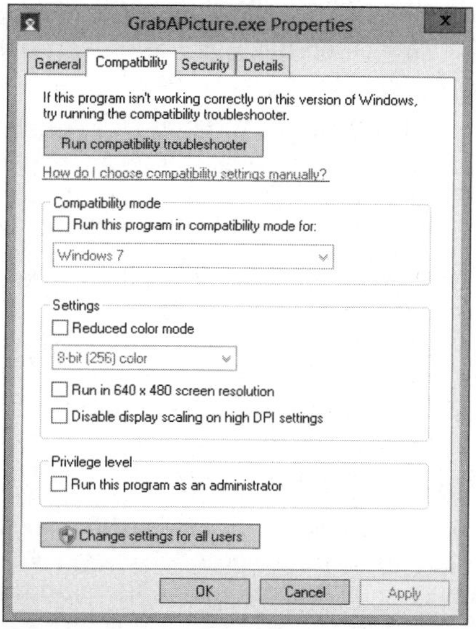

**Figure 3-14**

The settings shown in this list help you create an environment in which the application can run in most cases. The environment only mimics the original application environment, so the changes may not work. In addition, you may find that certain application features work well, but others don't because Windows 8 stores data in a different place or because other changes have nothing to do with the environment. The following list provides an overview of the changes you can make to create a compatible environment:

- ✔ **Compatibility Mode:** Each version of Windows has provided a slightly different application environment. This setting lets you tell Windows 8 to provide an environment similar to those previous versions of Windows for the application in question. You can choose many older versions of Windows, from Windows 95 through Windows 7.

- ✔ **Settings:** Certain ancient applications don't run well with modern hardware or with the capabilities that modern hardware has to offer. The following suboptions help you create an environment that better mimics the hardware used by older systems:

  - • **Reduced Color Mode:** Modifies the environment to provide fewer color choices.

  - • **Run in 640 × 480 Screen Resolution:** Configures Windows 8 to provide a 640 x 480 screen resolution. Use this setting when the application appears garbled when you run it.

  - • **Disable Display Scaling On High DPI Settings:** Creates an environment where Windows doesn't resize the application automatically to adapt it to the requirements of high dots-per-inch (DPI) font settings.

- ✔ **Privilege Level:** Some applications assume that you have administrator rights when you run them. The User Account Control (UAC) runs all applications with reduced rights for security reasons. This setting automatically elevates your privileges whenever you run the application.

## Revising settings for all users

Any change you make to the compatibility settings in an application normally affects only your session. Whenever you start Windows, the changes you've made take effect and the application runs as normal. However, figuring out the correct settings and then not sharing with others on your machine usually means that every person has to figure out the compatibility settings individually. To make the settings available to everyone, you must have an administrator account. You can then click Change Settings for All Users at the bottom of the Compatibility tab in the application's Properties dialog box to make the settings available to everyone on that machine.

# *Uninstalling Applications*

At some point, you may find that you no longer want an application installed on your system. Perhaps you've simply grown tired of it or you no longer need it to perform useful tasks. Whatever the reason, you no longer need the application. When working with applications that you've downloaded and haven't installed with an installer, all you need to do is remove any places where you've pinned the application, archive the data in case you need it later, and then delete the application folder (along with any data you created).

When an application appears in the Programs and Features applet of the Control Panel, however, you must uninstall the application properly. Otherwise, it can leave behind all sorts of remnants, and Windows can eventually become unstable. Use these steps to install any application that's registered as part of the Programs and Features applet:

1.  **Press Win+C.**

    You see the Charms bar.

2.  **Click the Settings charm.**

    You see the Settings page.

3.  **Click Control Panel.**

    You see the Control Panel displayed.

4.  **Click Uninstall a Program (under the Programs heading).**

    Windows presents a list of applications installed on your system.

5.  **Select the application you want to uninstall and then click Uninstall on the applet's Taskbar.**

Windows starts the uninstall process. In some cases, you must answer questions about the application installation, such as whether to save your personal data files or to delete them as part of the uninstall process.

# Working with Gadgets

A *gadget* is a bit of code that performs one or two tasks. Gadgets normally appear in a special place on your Desktop, and Windows 8 comes packaged with a number of these gadgets. For example, you have access to a Clock gadget that tells you the time and a Weather gadget that can tell you today's weather.

The gadgets that come with Windows 8 comprise only the tip of the iceberg. You can easily download new gadgets, created by other people, to enhance your computing experience. When you tire of using a gadget, you simply remove it from your Desktop. Later, you can add the gadget again when you decide that you need it. This part tells you all about gadgets and describes how these little bits of code can provide useful functionality.

## In this part . . .

- ✓ **Adding Gadgets to the Desktop**
- ✓ **Eliminating Gadgets from the Desktop**
- ✓ **Obtaining New Gadgets**

# Adding Gadgets to the Desktop

Gadgets aren't actually new to Windows 8. They originally appeared as part of Windows Vista and continued to provide functionality as part of Windows 7. The Windows 8 change for gadgets is that they appear as standalone icons on the Desktop and you can move them around — an improvement over the use of the Windows Sidebar to hold gadgets in earlier versions of Windows. The gadgets that Microsoft provides as part of its operating system haven't changed much, either. The following sections explain how to make gadgets appear on the Desktop and then describe each standard gadget in detail.

## Making gadgets appear on the Desktop

By default, Windows 8 doesn't install gadgets on your Desktop. To use a gadget, you must first tell the operating system to add it to the Desktop. The following steps describe how to perform this task:

1. **Right-click the Desktop and choose Gadgets from the context menu.**

    Windows displays a list of gadgets installed on the system in the Gadget Gallery, as shown in Figure 4-1. (This is the default list of gadgets.)

Figure 4-1

2. **Double-click any gadget in the list.**

    As an example, click the Clock gadget. You see the Clock gadget appear on the Desktop, as shown in Figure 4-2.

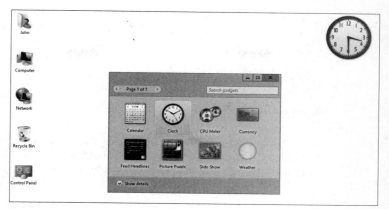

Figure 4-2

## Using the Calendar gadget

The Calendar gadget is simply a calendar you can keep at your fingertips. Sometimes, you don't really need to record anything; all you need to know is what the day of the week is or how many days until a specific date. The Calendar gadget mimics a paper calendar in that you can thumb through it quickly to see how a date might work out. The default view shows the current date. (See Figure 4-3.)

Figure 4-3

Double-clicking the Calendar gadget shows the month view. (See Figure 4-4.) Notice that the current date is shown in a different color and that you can use the arrows at the top of the calendar to view other months.

**Figure 4-4**

Most gadgets support a number of supplementary features. The Calendar gadget supports the supplementary features described in the following sections. The information described in these sections also applies to any gadget that supports that feature.

### Adjusting the size of gadgets

You may not want to switch between the individual day view and the month view. The Calendar gadget provides a larger size that shows both views simultaneously. To use this mode, simply move the mouse to the right side of the display to show a list of icons. Locate the Larger icon and click it. You see a larger view of the gadget, as shown in Figure 4-5. Click the Smaller icon to restore the smaller gadget size.

**Figure 4-5**

As an alternative to using the menu on the right side of the gadget, you can right-click the gadget to display a context menu. Choose Size⇨Small Size or Size⇨Large Size as needed to resize the gadget.

### Moving gadgets

Gadgets always appear in the upper-right corner of the display when you start them. Of course, that might not be a convenient location for the gadget, so you can move it as needed. To move a gadget, move the mouse to the right side of the display to show a list of icons. Locate the Move icon at the bottom of the list and use it to drag the gadget wherever you want. As an alternative to using the menu, you can right-click the gadget and choose Move from the context menu. The mouse cursor turns into a four-sided arrow, and you can drag the gadget wherever you want.

### Preserving gadgets on top

The gadgets you select normally remain on the Desktop, out of the way until you need to use them. However, you can choose to keep the gadget on top of everything so that it's always available. To select this option, right-click the gadget and choose Always On Top from the context menu. The gadget now appears as the topmost window. If you later decide that you really don't want to see the gadget all the time, right-click the gadget again and clear the check next to Always On Top.

### Setting gadget opacity

The *opacity* of a gadget determines whether you can see through it. Normally, a gadget is *opaque,* which means that it hides anything behind it. When you change the gadget's opacity setting, you make it possible to see items behind the gadget. To change a gadget's opacity, right-click the gadget and choose an option from the Opacity submenu.

## Using the Clock gadget

The Clock gadget shows the current time by default using a clock that looks like it might be in a school or factory. (See Figure 4-6.) As with the Calendar gadget, you can change the position of the Clock and tell Windows to display it on top of any other windows. In addition, you can set the opacity of the Clock.

Figure 4-6

The Clock gadget is a little more complex than the Calendar gadget. In this case, you have access to a number of options that control how the Clock works. The following section describes how gadget options generally work and explains specifically how the Clock gadget works.

## Setting gadget options

Some gadgets provide options that let you control their behavior. To access this feature, either right-click the gadget and choose Options from the context menu or move the mouse cursor to the right and choose the Options icon from the gadget's menu. For example, the Clock supports a number of options that help you modify its appearance, give it a name, and even change its time zone. (See Figure 4-7.)

**Figure 4-7**

By clicking the left or right arrow at the top, you can change the appearance of the Clock. The Clock Name field lets you use multiple clocks to keep track of time in other places. The Time Zone field lets you choose any time zone from around the world. Finally, it's possible to display the second hand on the Clock by selecting the Show the Second Hand option.

When working with a gadget like Clock, you may need to open more than one copy. Configure each copy differently so that you can track time from various time zones where you work. Use this approach to avoid having to guess what time it is in California when you work in New York.

## Using the CPU Meter gadget

The CPU Meter shows a quick view of your processor and memory usage, as shown in Figure 4-8. The larger of the two meters shows processor usage, and the smaller meter shows memory usage. This gadget provides both small and large sizes (as shown in the figure) so that you can see the readings more easily.

Figure 4-8

## Using the Currency gadget

The Currency gadget helps you convert from one currency to another. To use this gadget, you select one currency in the top drop-down list box and the currency you want to convert to in the bottom drop-down list box. Then you type the currency amount you want to convert in the upper text box. For example, Currency is converting between US$100 and the euro in Figure 4-9. Fortunately, this gadget supports a larger size so that you can actually see the values.

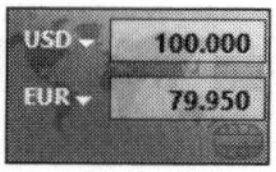

Figure 4-9

## Using the Feed Headlines gadget

All other standard gadgets start up in a way that lets you use them immediately. Feed Headlines starts in a dormant state. The following steps help you configure this gadget:

*1.* **Locate a site that contains a Really Simple Syndication (RSS) feed you want to see.**

Any site that provides this feature displays an orange-and-white RSS icon. Many place the words *Subscribe by RSS* next to the icon.

2. **Click the RSS icon.**

   A new page opens, where you can see a description of the feed.

3. **Click the subscription link, which is normally labeled Subscribe to This Feed.**

   Internet Explorer displays the Subscribe to This Feed dialog box, as shown in Figure 4-10.

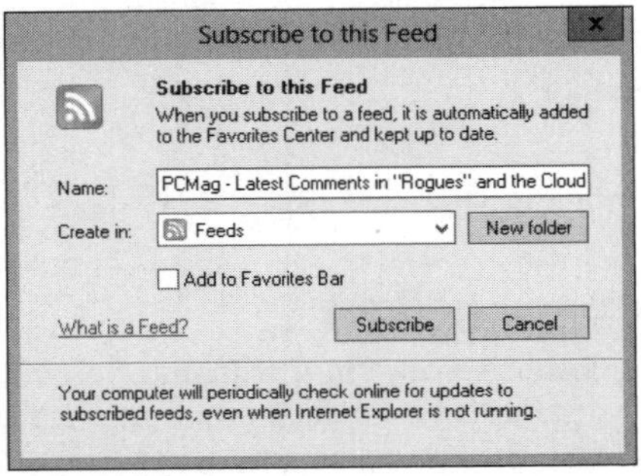

**Figure 4-10**

4. **Start Feed Headlines as you would start any other gadget.**

   You see the gadget appear onscreen.

5. **Right-click Feed Headlines and choose Options from the context menu.**

   You see the Feed Headlines dialog box, as shown in Figure 4-11.

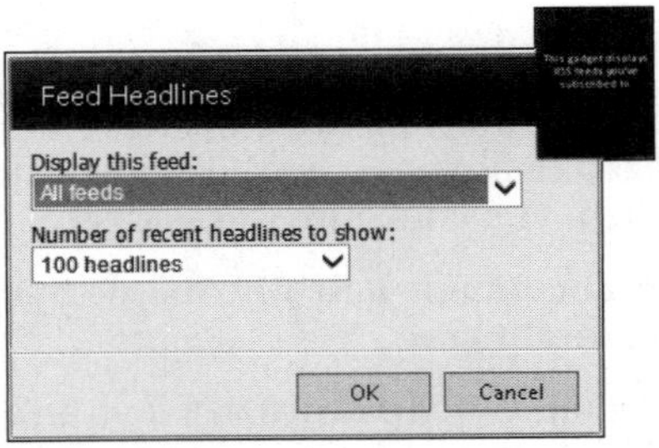

**Figure 4-11**

6. **Choose the feeds you want to see from the Display This Feed list.**

7. **Select the number of headlines you want to see for each feed in the Number of Recent Headlines to Show list and then click OK.**

   Feed Headlines shows a list of the headlines you selected, as shown in Figure 4-12.

**Figure 4-12**

Click any feeds you want to see. The feed content appears in a small window to the left of the gadget so that you can read it. As with a few other gadgets, this gadget supports both small and large sizes so that you can more easily read the headings.

## Using the Picture Puzzle gadget

Picture Puzzle is a fun gadget. It places an image on tiles that it then scrambles. Move the tiles around until the picture is unscrambled. You can't resize this gadget to make it larger, but the options let you choose from a number of images.

## Using the Slideshow gadget

The Slideshow gadget is one of the few that has a Start screen corollary. By itself, the gadget displays a series of pictures onscreen for you to enjoy as you work. When you open the options by right-clicking the gadget (see Figure 4-13), you can choose where to obtain pictures, specify how long to display them, and make other choices.

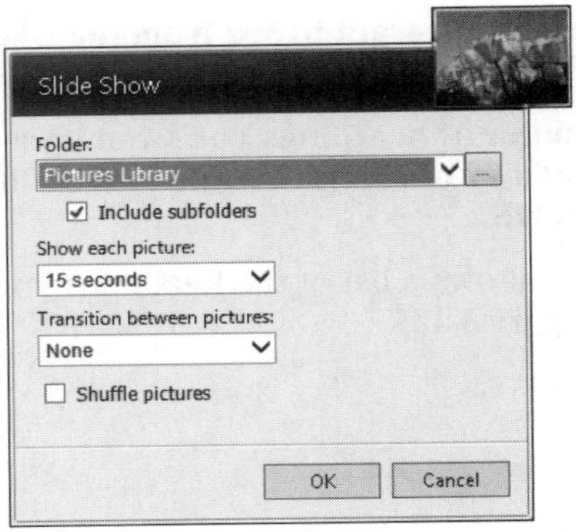

**Figure 4-13**

The gadget supports a small or large size, along with all the usual options. However, something special happens when you hover the mouse over the gadget: A set of controls appears on the gadget itself (along with the usual icons on the right side), as shown in Figure 4-14.

**Figure 4-14**

These controls let you choose how to display the images. The leftmost control takes you to the beginning of the image list, the second starts or stops the automatic display of the next image in the list, and the third takes you to the end of the list. However, the fourth button, View, is the most interesting. Click this button and Windows automatically opens the Photos app so that you can see the full-screen view of a particular image.

## Using the Weather gadget

The Weather gadget shows the current weather at whatever location you choose by using the Options dialog box. In fact, you can open several Weather gadgets to display weather from different locations. In this case, you can tell the basic weather conditions by viewing the icon as well. For example, you see the sun shining when the sky is clear. However, the small view of this particular gadget is limited. The large view (see Figure 4-15) is a lot more interesting and informative.

**Figure 4-15**

Now you can see the three-day forecast for a particular area and today's high and low temperature, along with the current temperature. The images associated with the forecast give you an indicator of the weather for that timeframe. Click this gadget and it opens a copy of Internet Explorer that takes you to a more detailed weather report.

# Eliminating Gadgets from the Desktop

Gadgets, like any other Windows feature, can become overwhelming when you overuse them. At some point, you may decide that you need to remove one or more gadgets to make space for something else. You have two options for removing gadgets:

- Temporarily remove the gadget by right-clicking it and choosing Close Gadget from the context menu or by clicking the Close icon on the gadget's menu.

- Permanently uninstall the gadget by right-clicking its entry in the Gadget Gallery and choosing Uninstall from the context menu.

The second option is permanent only because you need to reinstall the gadget before you can use it again. Because gadgets are incredibly small pieces of code, the first option of temporarily removing the gadget from the Desktop is normally the best idea.

# Obtaining New Gadgets

A gadget is actually quite useful in some cases, and developers have spent quite a bit of time coming up with unique ideas for using its small form factor. You can find a number of Microsoft gadgets for your Windows 8 setup at `http://windows.`

`microsoft.com/en-US/windows/downloads/personalize/` `gadgets`. In addition to Microsoft's support, a number of sites provide access to gadgets or plan to support Windows 8–specific gadgets soon. For example, you can find Windows 8 gadgets at `http://windows8gadgets.net`.

The gadgets you can download run the gamut in functionality. For example, you can download a gadget to help you partici- pate in online auctions or track the remaining power level in your laptop battery. Here's what you do to get a new gadget installed on your machine:

*1.* **Click the Download link.**

Internet Explorer asks whether you want to open or save the file.

*2.* **Choose Open.**

The file downloads to your system and automatically starts to install. You see the Security Warning dialog box.

*3.* **Click Install.**

The gadget appears in the Gadget Gallery and automati- cally displays on the Desktop, where you can configure it.

# Using Internet Explorer

The speed at which browser technology has changed over the years is amazing. What originally was an application used to view static content is now used to run fully interactive applications from remote locations and to view dynamic content in myriad ways. The threats to your browser have also increased in proportion to the functionality it can provide. To keep up, browser designers create new techniques for detecting and thwarting threats as they become issues. This part helps you understand the new capabilities that Internet Explorer provides, along with the increased potential it has for keeping your computer safe. The balance between functionality and safety is an important one to grasp as you work with the latest version of Internet Explorer provided with Windows 8.

There are actually two versions of Internet Explorer with Windows 8: the Start screen version and the Desktop version. The Start screen version doesn't allow for add-ins, cannot use Adobe Flash, and doesn't support Java. The Desktop version is significantly more capable and works more like older versions of Internet Explorer. The trade-off between the two is that the Start screen version of Internet Explorer is more secure. This part focuses on the Desktop version of Internet Explorer, but the procedures will work equally well with either version.

## In this part . . .

- ✔ Knowing Where You Go
- ✔ Making Internet Explorer Configuration Changes
- ✔ Managing Add-Ons
- ✔ Using the Safety Features

# *Knowing Where You Go*

Most users now rely on content from hundreds of sites. Not all those sites are used every day. In fact, some are used only once or twice. Even so, knowing where you go and what you find there are essential if you want to determine how to access that information again. Internet Explorer provides three methods of tracking information sources:

- **Favorites:** Use the list of favorites to categorize and save locations you visit often.

- **Feeds:** Use feeds for information that you want sent automatically to your browser, e-mail application, or Feed Headlines gadget. (See the "Using the Feed Headlines gadget" section of Part 4.)

- **History:** Rely on history to tell you about places you've visited recently that you don't plan to revisit often.

If these three methods sound familiar, it's because they're part of previous releases of Internet Explorer. Microsoft is always trying to find ways to tweak these features to make them easier to use, so you might be surprised at the way seemingly minor changes make your life easier. The following sections describe these features in more detail.

## Accessing favorites

Your list of *favorite* sites presents a list of content sources that you use most often. (You create this list manually by using the procedure that appears later in this section.) It doesn't matter what sort of content you use. A favorite provides the means to access that content quickly and easily.

As with any application feature, it's possible to get too much of a good thing with favorites. To quickly access the content you want, you need to categorize it. The favorites you keep should also present sources that you use often. When you fill your favorites list with links that you use seldom (if ever), it makes it harder to find the link you really want. Keeping the links current is also important because sites continually change their locations and old links that don't point to anything simply clutter your favorites list.

Before you can access any favorites, you must create a list of them. Use the following procedure to add a new favorite to your list:

***1.*** **Click View Favorites, Feeds, and History (the star icon in the upper-right corner of Internet Explorer) or press Alt+C.**

You see the drop-down list shown in Figure 5-1.

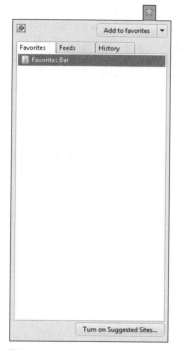

**Figure 5-1**

***2.*** **Click Add to Favorites.**

You see the Add a Favorite dialog box, as shown in Figure 5-2.

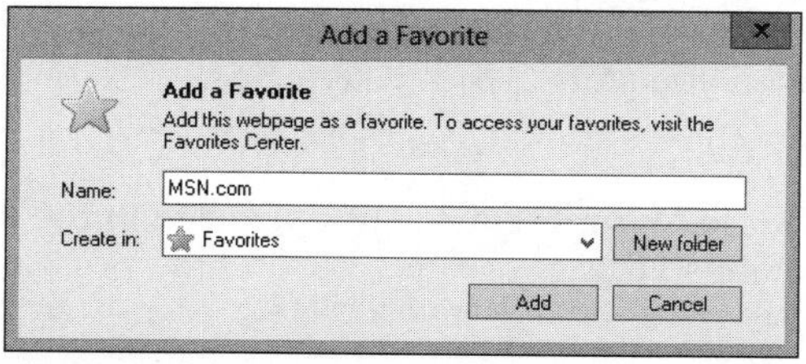

**Figure 5-2**

3. **(Optional) Type a name for the favorite in the Name field.**

    Many people use the site-provided name for the favorite. In some cases, the name isn't descriptive, so you need to think about whether you can identify the site based on its default name. Sometimes, supplementary information is helpful.

4. **(Optional) Choose a folder to use to store the favorite.**

    If you don't choose a folder, Internet Explorer stores the favorite in the root folder. Using the root folder for all your favorites can quickly become a mess. It helps to create a folder, when necessary, using the following procedure.

    When creating a favorite, you can place it on the Favorites bar, which appears when you click the down arrow in the Address field of the browser. Use this option only when you work with a favorite every time you use Internet Explorer.

    a. *Click New Folder.*

       You see the Create a Folder dialog box, as shown in Figure 5-3.

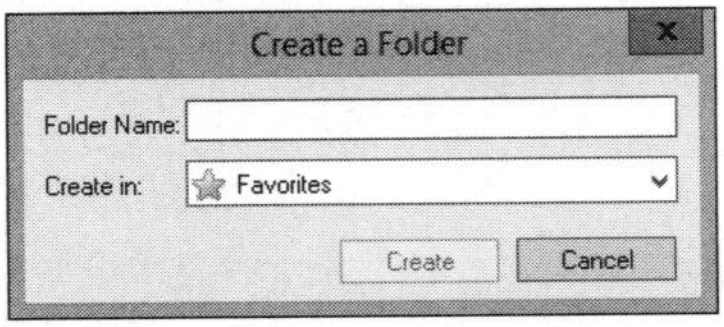

    | Create a Folder | X |
    |---|---|
    | Folder Name: | |
    | Create in: ⭐ Favorites | ⌄ |
    | | Create | Cancel |

**Figure 5-3**

    b. *Type a name for the folder in the Folder Name field.*

    c. *Choose a parent folder for the folder in the Create In field and then click Create.*

       The default parent folder is named Favorites. In fact, this is the only folder you can use as a parent folder when you start creating favorites.

5. **Click Add.**

    Internet Explorer creates a new favorite in the location you requested.

You access your favorites in one of two ways: items on the Favorites bar and other items. When working with favorites on the Favorites bar, click the down arrow in the Address field, as shown in Figure 5-4. The *Favorites bar* is the list of items in the Favorites section of this drop-down list.

| http://az155373.vo.msecnd.net/webslices/ie9?culture=en-us | | |
| --- | --- | --- |
| History | | |
| Personalize Your Web Brows... | http://az15537... | Shift + Enter |
| MSN.com | | |
| Favorites | | |
| Web Slice Gallery | | |
| MSN.com | | |
| | | Add |

**Figure 5-4**

When you need to access other favorites, click View Favorites, Feeds, and History or press Alt+C. Open any of the folders that you created to hold favorites, and click the link you want to see.

## Accessing feeds

*Really Simple Syndication (RSS) feeds* provide the means for pushing information out to browsers instead of requiring the browser to request the information. For example, you use an RSS feed to keep track of a news event or a discussion. As people add new content to the feed site, you see it in your browser automatically. The "Using the Feed Headlines gadget" section of Part 4 tells you how to create feeds by clicking the standard orange-and-white RSS icon.

Most people use a special RSS reader to work with RSS feeds. Often, this reader is part of an e-mail application. Windows 8 also provides access to RSS feeds through the Feed Headlines gadget. If neither of these options appeals to you, you can always view a feed directly in Internet Explorer by clicking View Favorites, Feeds, and History or pressing Alt+C and selecting the Feeds tab. (See Figure 5-5.)

**Figure 5-5**

You click the feed link to view it. When you hover the mouse over the link, you see information about the feed in a tooltip, such as the last time it received an update. (Refer to Figure 5-5.)

## Reviewing history

Internet Explorer tracks the places you visit on the Internet. This historical information makes it possible to go back to a site that you plan to visit only once or twice, without having to store the link as a favorite. You don't do anything special to record this information — Internet Explorer does it automatically for you. (See the "Deleting the browsing history" section, later in this part, to find out how to remove this information automatically when you close the browser.)

By default, Internet Explorer stores the history by date, but it also provides other methods of sorting the information, such as by most-visited site. To see your browsing history, click View Favorites, Feeds, and History or press Alt+C and then select the History tab. (See Figure 5-6.) Double-click Today to open the list of links associated with today's browsing sessions.

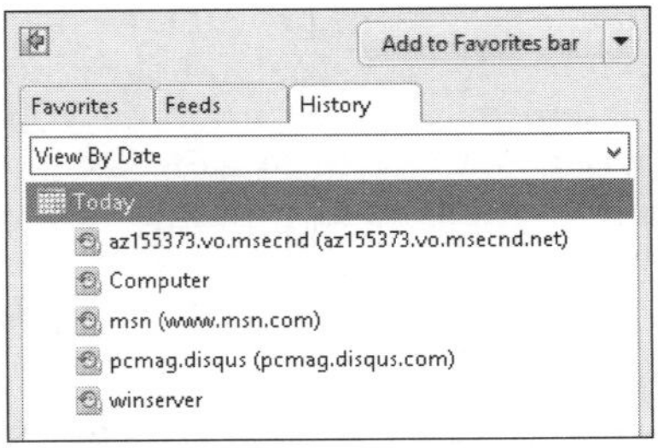

**Figure 5-6**

Select any existing link by clicking it, as you would select any favorite. The drop-down list at the top of the window provides various methods of sorting links and making a particular link easier to find.

# Making Internet Explorer Configuration Changes

Internet Explorer provides a host of configuration options. These options do everything from ensuring that you can connect to the Internet properly to ensuring that your system and identity remain safe. To see the configuration options, click Tools (the gear icon) in the upper-right corner of Internet Explorer or press Alt+X. Select Internet Options from the menu. You see the Internet Options dialog box, which contains a number of tabs. The following sections describe the various Internet Explorer configuration options on these tabs and explain how to use them.

## Setting the General options

The General tab contains a number of options that don't quite fit anywhere else. For example, you use this tab to change the home page in Internet Explorer, as shown in Figure 5-7. The *home page* determines the starting location that Internet Explorer uses every time it starts. In this case, the home page is about:blank, which is a safe, blank page that loads instantaneously (because it contains nothing).

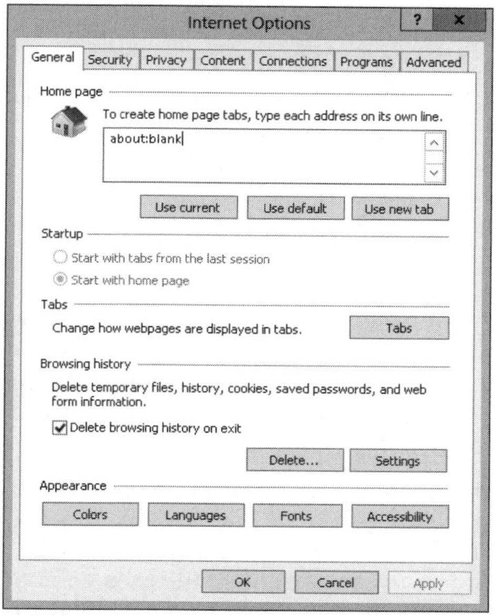

**Figure 5-7**

When you choose to maintain the historical information that Internet Explorer gathers, you can also choose whether to start with a home page or with the same tabs you had open the last session. If you choose to start with the same tabs you had open during the last session, Internet Explorer ignores any home page information you provide.

Internet Explorer supports the use of tabs so that you can have multiple pages open at one time. The tab settings control how tabs work when you use them. Click Tabs to see the settings shown in Figure 5-8.

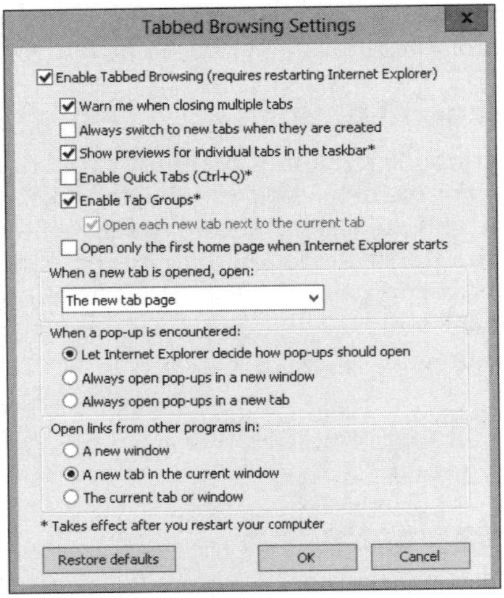

**Tabbed Browsing Settings** ✕

☑ Enable Tabbed Browsing (requires restarting Internet Explorer)
  ☑ Warn me when closing multiple tabs
  ☐ Always switch to new tabs when they are created
  ☑ Show previews for individual tabs in the taskbar*
  ☐ Enable Quick Tabs (Ctrl+Q)*
  ☑ Enable Tab Groups*
    ☑ Open each new tab next to the current tab
  ☐ Open only the first home page when Internet Explorer starts
When a new tab is opened, open:

> The new tab page      ∨

When a pop-up is encountered:
  ◉ Let Internet Explorer decide how pop-ups should open
  ○ Always open pop-ups in a new window
  ○ Always open pop-ups in a new tab

Open links from other programs in:
  ○ A new window
  ◉ A new tab in the current window
  ○ The current tab or window

* Takes effect after you restart your computer

[ Restore defaults ]      [ OK ] [ Cancel ]

**Figure 5-8**

By default, Internet Explorer enables tabbed browsing to provide you with the most flexible experience possible. Clearing the Enable Tabbed Browsing check box and restarting Internet Explorer disables tabbed browsing, which means that you see one page at a time. However, this loss of flexibility also creates a gain in performance, so you may decide to disable tabbed browsing when memory resources on your machine are low.

When you enable tabs, the remaining options control how the tabs appear and work onscreen. For example, the Quick Tabs feature tells Internet Explorer to provide *thumbnails* (little pictures showing the site content) of all the tabs you have open at any given time. You can view the thumbnails by pressing Ctrl+Q or clicking the Quick Tabs icon. Clicking a thumbnail takes you to that tab.

It's essential to look for an asterisk (*) after any option you check or select. The asterisk spells out a special condition that you must meet before the condition modified by the option occurs. For example, you must restart your machine before

Internet Explorer will enable or disable Quick Tabs. You can modify the setting all you want, but Internet Explorer's behavior doesn't change until you restart the system. You can easily overlook an asterisk, so look closely to ensure that you understand the conditions required to make a change.

The Tabbed Browsing Settings dialog box also controls how pop-ups appear. (*Pop-ups* are message box-like windows that appear with additional content.) For example, you can choose to open pop-ups in a new tab. Likewise, you can control how links from other programs work. The default setting opens these links in a new tab in the existing window, but you can choose to open the link in a new window or in the existing tab instead.

The General tab of the Options dialog box contains a few other interesting features. The options in the Browsing History area are actually security features that you can use to keep your sessions safer. The "Deleting the browsing history" section, later in this part, provides more information about these features.

The Appearance area of the dialog box contains controls that make pages easier to see and use, especially for anyone with special needs. For example, some sites use type so small that I can't see it, so I override the site's type settings and use my own. Sometimes, this action results in pages that don't look quite the way the author intended, but at least I can see the content. The color options ensure that anyone who has trouble seeing various color combinations can avoid them, for the most part. In fact, you can even create and use your own Cascading Style Sheet (CSS) file to fully control how a site appears and then use the options in the Accessibility dialog box (click Accessibility to see it) to enforce your style choices.

## Setting the Security options

Internet Explorer relies on zone-based security. Each site you open resides in a specific zone. The default setting for anything on the Internet is the Internet zone. The four zones are Internet (anything online), Local Intranet (your local network), Trusted Sites (local resources and special sites that you tell Internet Explorer are safe), and Restricted Sites (any place you that do not trust), as shown in Figure 5-9.

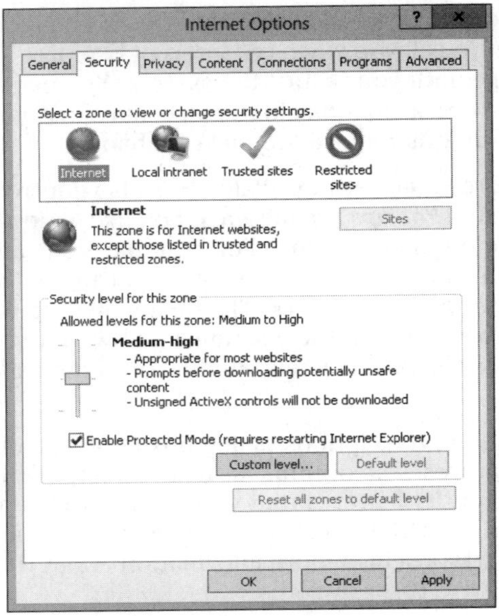

Figure 5-9

Each zone provides individualized security settings. The basic means to set the security level is the slider that appears in the middle of the dialog box. When you decide that you want to create special security setups, you can click Custom Level to display the individual security options and choose which options the zone will use.

Using zones for particular purposes is automatic. When you choose a location on your local network, Internet Explorer automatically uses the Local Intranet zone for it. However, you can also choose to relax security (Trusted Sites zone) or to increase it (Restricted Sites zone) for specific sites. Click Sites after selecting one of these two zones to display a dialog box like the one shown in Figure 5-10.

Even though Figure 5-10 shows the Trusted Sites zone, both zones work about the same way, except that the Restricted Sites zone doesn't require server verification. To add a site to either the Trusted Sites or Restricted Sites zone, type the URL for the site in the Add This Website to the Zone field and click Add.

Notice that the Trusted Sites zone requires URLs with the HyperText Transfer Protocol Secure (https) protocol by default. You can clear the Require Server Verification (https:)

for All Sites in This Zone check box to use regular (nonverified) URLs. Adding regular sites to your Trusted Sites zone is exceptionally dangerous, and you should do it only when you're absolutely certain that no danger exists.

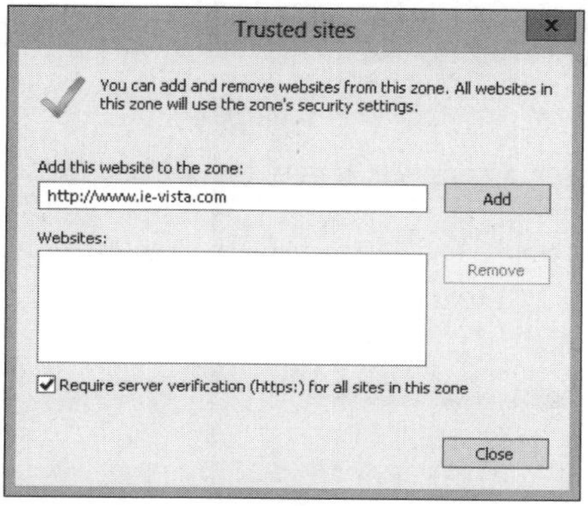

**Figure 5-10**

It pays to be a little paranoid about security. The Internet zone and Restricted Sites zone have the Enable Protected Mode option selected by default. Protected mode provides enhanced security features for Internet Explorer, and using this mode in all zones isn't a bad idea. You can learn more about Protected mode at http://msdn.microsoft.com/library/bb250462.aspx.

## Setting the Privacy options

Everyone is spying on you! When you go to various sites, they add cookies (or another means of tracking you) to your system. The number of ways in which sites perform this task is amazing. In many cases, such as when you visit Amazon.com, the site tracks you to obtain marketing information and to offer suggestions on purchases you may want. However, sites have many other reasons to track you — some of which aren't very nice.

It's the best practice today to avoid having someone track you, if at all possible. Unfortunately, not allowing a site to track you can cause the site to malfunction, so you often have to choose between site functionality and keeping your privacy intact. The default Internet Explorer setting, which appears on the Privacy tab (see Figure 5-11), provides a sort of middle ground that offers a decent level of usefulness without compromising your privacy too much.

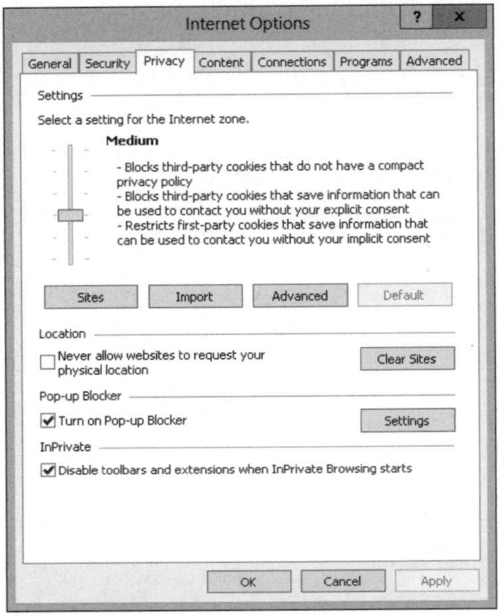

**Figure 5-11**

The settings tell Internet Explorer to reject cookies that don't provide a privacy policy and that can be used for reasons other than offering purchase suggestions or obtaining marketing information. For some people, even this level of tracking is too much, so you need to increase the privacy setting.

No matter where you specify the privacy setting, it's still up to you to read the site's privacy policy and determine whether you agree with it. (See the "Finding out the web page privacy policy" section, later in this part, for details.) In some cases, you won't agree with the privacy policy because it gives the site too much control or offers too much access to your information. Then you can choose to modify the privacy setting for that site by clicking Sites. You see the Per Site Privacy Actions dialog box, as shown in Figure 5-12.

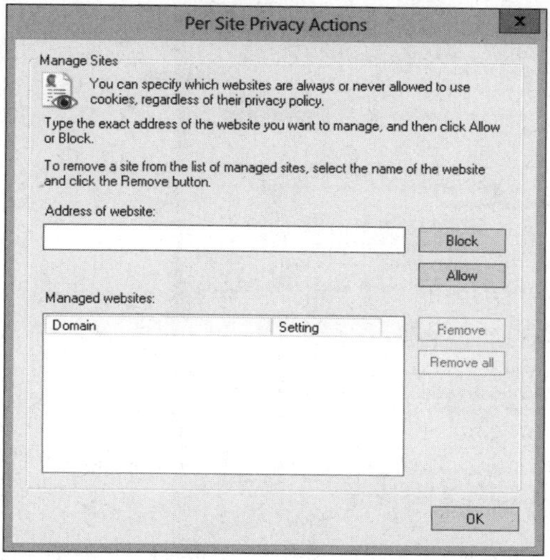

**Figure 5-12**

Type the URL for the site you want to manage, and click either Block (to block all cookies) or Allow (to allow all cookies). The site will appear in the list with its status (blocked or allowed). Using the Per Site Privacy Actions dialog box allows you to keep the general privacy policy at a high level while allowing sites you trust to store cookies as needed.

The Privacy tab also provides settings for location information, pop-ups, and add-on toolbars and extensions. All these Internet Explorer features can compromise your privacy when used incorrectly. As with cookies, you can set pop-up policy on a site-by-site basis.

## Setting the Content options

The Content tab contains settings that affect the presentation of content within Internet Explorer. Content can involve a wide variety of issues, as shown in Figure 5-13.

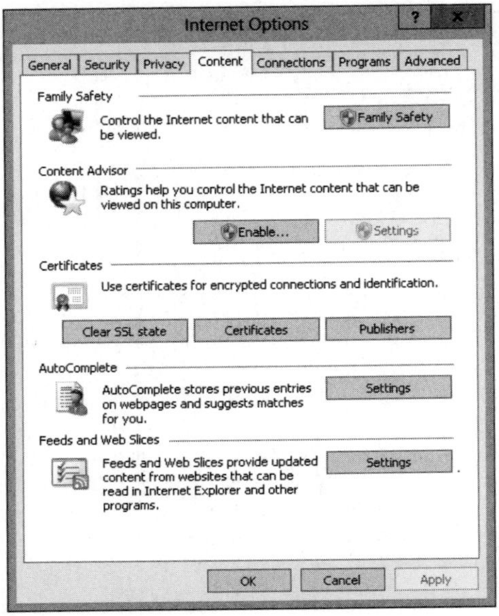

**Figure 5-13**

At the top of the dialog box, you see Family Safety and Content Advisor sections. Both features provide a safe environment in which to view content. The first one, Family Safety, restricts access to less desirable sites when children are involved. The second, Content Advisor, blocks sites based on the sort of content they contain. For example, you can choose to block sites that contain nudity or inappropriate language. You can read about various Internet content ratings systems at www.efa.org.au/Issues/Censor/cens2a.html.

In the middle of the Content tab, you see options for working with certificates. A *certificate* is a digital identity. You can have a certificate that positively identifies you as a certain individual as verified by a third party, such as VeriSign. Content publishers (online sites) can also have certificates that positively identify them. Again, a third party verifies the publisher's identity so that you don't need to worry about someone fooling you. To make the certificates work, you must use a secure protocol (such as https) to communicate with the site. The company that issues your certificate can tell you a lot more about how certificates work. You can obtain a good overview of this topic at http://technet.microsoft.com/library/cc940384.aspx.

*AutoComplete* is an interesting feature because it attempts to predict what you'll type next. As Internet Explorer builds a history of your usage patterns, it can begin predicting what you'll type next, based on what you've typed in the past. This feature can help you find content faster because you type less information to access it. In addition, unless you've made mistakes in the past, using this feature can reduce the number of typos you make.

The last area on the Content tab helps you manage feeds and Web Slices. You can perform tasks such as telling Internet Explorer how often each day to update feeds. Previous sections in this part and in Part 4 discuss the RSS feed (essentially, a mechanism for pushing information to your machine so that you can see updates in real time). A *Web Slice* is a related technology that relies on RSS to allow you to subscribe to a particular part of a page. The Web Slice provides automatic updates to that portion of the page as needed to keep the content updated. You can read more about Web Slice technology at `http://msdn.microsoft.com/library/windows/desktop/cc956158.aspx`.

## Setting the Connections options

Before you can view *any* content, you must have a connection to a content source. Modern computers normally rely on the Internet to perform this task, but some systems also rely on a local intranet (your local network) to perform the task. The Connections tab, shown in Figure 5-14, contains settings that affect how Internet Explorer connects to outside sources (both Internet and intranet).

At some point in the dim past, users spent considerable time and effort attempting to make a connection using the settings on this tab. Internet Explorer has gotten so good at making connections that users rarely, if ever, even view this tab. In most cases, if you can't make a connection to the Internet, you need to contact your network administrator to obtain specific instructions on how to configure Internet Explorer for your network.

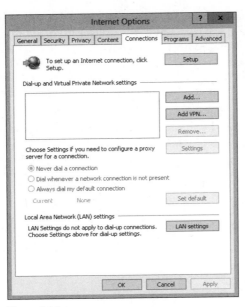

**Figure 5-14**

Trying to configure the options on the Connections tab can cause your system to lose a connection. It's far more likely for your DSL modem or another network device to require a reset than for Internet Explorer to require reconfiguration. Always try accessing the Internet from another system before you assume that you need to change the configuration settings. The only real exception to this rule is when you need to make a connection using a Virtual Private Network (VPN), in which case you do need to get the settings from your network administrator.

## Shaping the Programs options

The Programs tab (see Figure 5-15) contains options for configuring applications and other code that interacts with Internet Explorer in specific ways. For example, you can choose whether Internet Explore opens all links within the actual browser or sends some (or all) links to the Windows Desktop for display in tiles. To display content on the Desktop, you must select the Open Internet Explorer Tiles on the Desktop option.

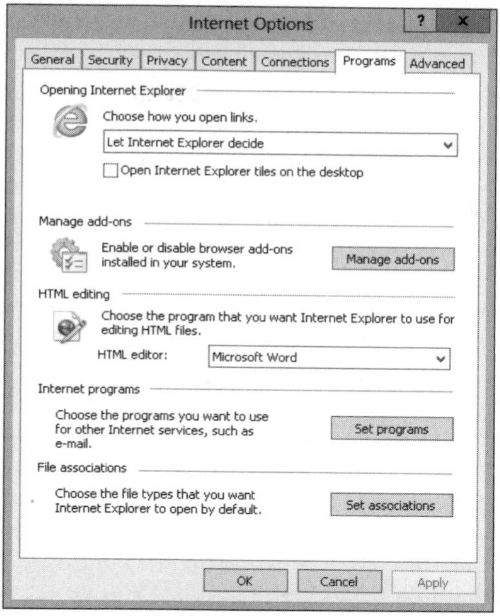

**Figure 5-15**

An add-on provides the means to extend Internet Explorer in a specific way. For example, the Shockwave Flash Object lets you play certain kinds of media using your browser. If you don't have this extension installed, the content is unplayable. The "Managing Add-Ons" section, later in this part, describes this topic in more detail.

When you work with content, you often need to edit the HTML that formats it. HTML also controls how the content works and adds functionality such as links. If you have Microsoft Word installed on your system, Internet Explorer defaults to using that editor for HTML content. Word provides several extremely useful HTML editing features. However, some people prefer to use Notepad because it loads quickly, consumes few resources, and provides the features needed for simple editing tasks. You may find that you have other potential HTML editors installed on your system as well.

The Internet Programs section of the tab helps you configure the applications used to work with content that Internet Explorer downloads from a remote location. For example, you can specify which application to use when a user clicks a PDF or ZIP file. It's also possible to configure AutoPlay events and describe which default applications to use for specific tasks, such as reading e-mail.

The final content issue that Internet Explorer must handle is knowing which programs handle specific content. In most cases, you want Internet Explorer to provide some level of application support for every kind of content it can handle. However, you might choose to use a different application to handle Scalable Vector Graphics (SVG) content, so you'd need to change that file association to use the right application. In most cases, you leave the file associations alone because Internet Explorer is the right application for the task.

## Working with the Advanced options

The Advanced tab (see Figure 5-16) contains a number of low-level options that affect how Internet Explorer performs tasks. In most cases, you don't modify these settings unless told to do so by product support or to address a particular need. For example, you may find that your hardware isn't up to the task of rendering (displaying) SVG content, so you could choose to use software rendering instead.

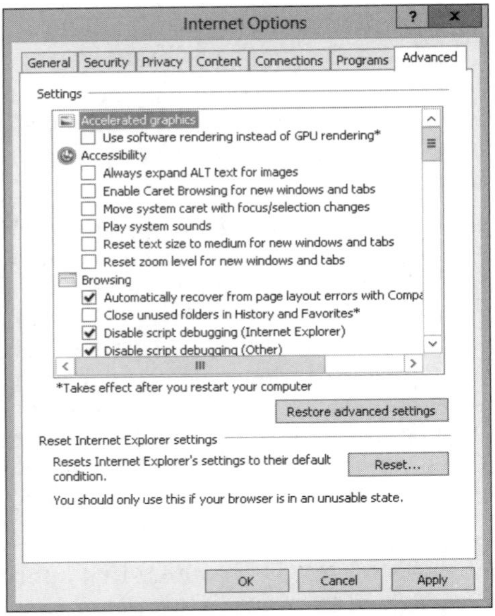

**Figure 5-16**

Internet Explorer categorizes these settings to make them easier to find. For example, all features that affect a user's ability to interact with Internet Explore appear in the Accessibility category.

Some users will need to scan the entire list to find every required settings change. Developers will find the settings that control script debugging in the Browsing category. However, the settings that control language features appear in the International category. In addition, developers usually need to test application security, and those features appear in the Security category.

Never change an advanced Internet Explorer option just to see what it does. Changing certain settings is quite dangerous and can result in damage to your system. For example, turning off the wrong security feature invites attack when you visit certain sites. In general, if you don't know what task the setting performs, leave it alone.

A number of sites online present ways of using the advanced settings to your advantage. For example, you can find an excellent article on setting practical security and privacy in Internet Explorer at `www.malwarehelp.org/configuring-internet-explorer1.html`. The Advanced tab settings appear at `www.malwarehelp.org/configuring-internet-explorer5.html`.

If you render your copy of Internet Explorer unusable or unsafe by making the wrong choices, you can always restore it to working condition by clicking Restore Advanced Settings. When Internet Explorer becomes unstable and restoring the advanced settings doesn't provide sufficient help, click Reset instead. Using these features causes your system to revert to its default state and causes you to lose any changes you made.

# Managing Add-Ons

An *add-on* makes it possible to extend the functionality of Internet Explorer in specific ways. For example, you can add a toolbar that makes it possible to interact with a site in a specific way or add tracking protection that helps you identify less reputable sites. You access the add-ons by clicking Manage Add-Ons on the Programs tab of the Internet Options dialog box. After you click Manage Add-Ons, you see the Manage Add-Ons dialog box.

WARNING

Add-ons can perform tasks that run counter to their intended purposes and actually *create* security breaches in your system. Some individuals will stoop to any means possible to gain access to your system, including the creation of Trojan applications. Always use add-ons with care and ensure that you know who the creator is before you install the add-on. One of the safest places to find add-ons for your system is at www.iegallery.com/ Addons.

The following sections describe several categories of add-ons and explain how these add-ons might help you use Internet Explorer more efficiently. Each add-on category has a specific task that it performs, and you should explore each one to find the kind of tool you require.

## Getting things done with toolbars and extensions

A *toolbar* provides additional user interface features, and an *extension* provides additional functionality. For example, a toolbar might provide easier access to a search provider or make it easier to locate specific kinds of information. A toolbar can help you perform tasks such as comparing the prices of products on different sites. An extension might let you play Flash files or display PDF files directly in Internet Explorer. The toolbars and extensions installed on your system appear in the Toolbars and Extensions folder of the Manage Add-Ons dialog box, as shown in Figure 5-17.

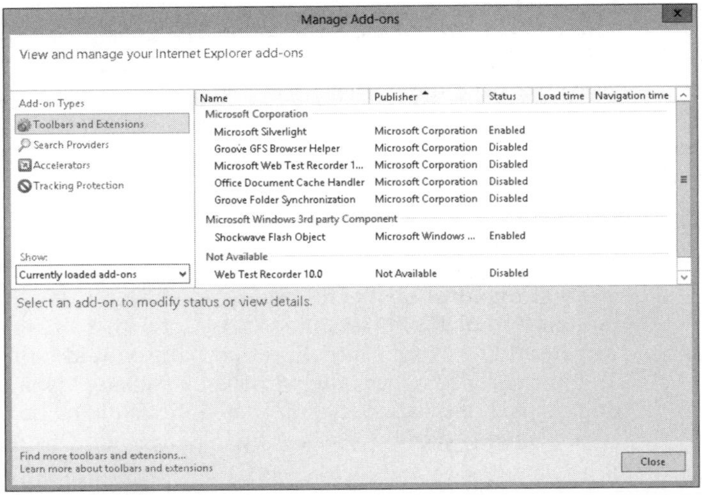

**Figure 5-17**

The Show drop-down list box helps you filter the add-ons list so it shows only the add-ons you want to see. In this case, you see just the loaded add-ons. If you want to see all add-ons, choose Add Add-Ons instead.

The list of toolbars and extensions includes the name of the toolbar or extension, the entity that created it, whether the add-on is enabled, whether the add-on is loaded (in use), and the amount of time it has been in use. Click a specific entry to see additional information about it. For example, you can discover the add-on's version number. The details area also provides a button for enabling or disabling the add-on and a link for locating additional information about the add-on.

## Managing search providers

You use a search provider to locate sites matching the criteria you specify. For example, when you want to look for scary books, you type *scary books* in the Address field, and Internet Explorer uses the search provider to display a list of scary books for you. Internet Explorer comes with a single default search provider, Bing, as shown in Figure 5-18. Note that the bottom half of the dialog box shows Bing details because Bing is selected.

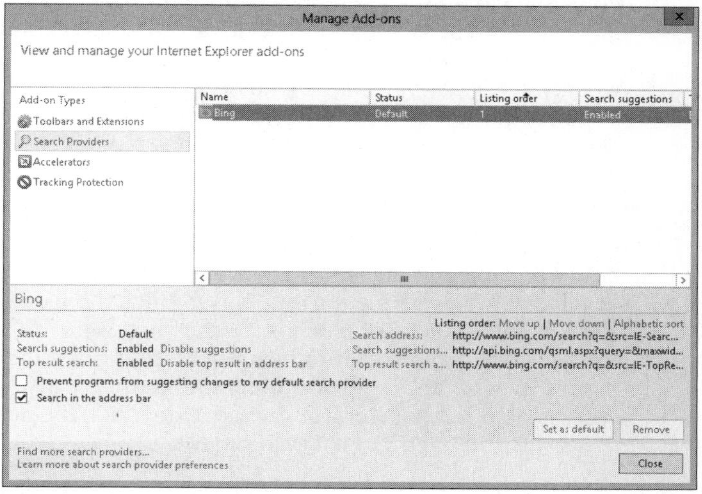

**Figure 5-18**

Many people use Bing and find everything they need. However, you may want to use another search provider or add a secondary search provider, for those times when Bing isn't successful. To add a new search provider, click Find More Search Providers. Internet Explorer opens a new window and displays a list of common search providers you can use. Click the search provider you want to use and then follow the simple directions to install it. As with many parts of Windows 8, you can start working immediately after selecting the new search provider. Windows 8 displays a *toast* (completion) message when it finishes installing the search provider for you.

One security feature found in Internet Explorer is the Prevent Programs from Suggesting Changes to My Default Search Provider option. Select this option to prevent applications from inadvertently changing your search provider — possibly to a search provider that redirects you to sites that will contaminate your system. When you're happy with the search results you obtain from your search provider, an application has no good reason to change the setting on you (and has many reasons not to change it).

## Setting up accelerators

*Accelerators* make accessing something fast. For example, when you have Flixter installed on your system, you can access information about actors and movies faster than if you had to search for the information first. Of course, accelerators are useful only when you regularly need the kind of access they provide. Internet Explorer comes with the x, y, and z accelerators by default, as shown in Figure 5-19. Notice that clicking the accelerator's name shows details about the accelerator in the bottom half of the dialog box.

Using an accelerator consists of highlighting a word or another entity on a page. You see a special icon telling you that an accelerator is available for that entity. Click the icon and you see a list of accelerator choices, as shown in Figure 5-20. Choose the accelerator you want to use. Notice that hovering the mouse over an accelerator option automatically displays the content that the accelerator can provide. Click the accelerator to see the full-page view of the content.

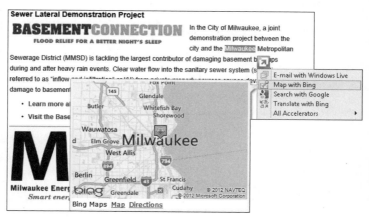

| Add-on Types | Name ▲ | Address | Category | Status |
|---|---|---|---|---|
| Toolbars and Extensions | Email | | | |
| Search Providers | E-mail with Windows Live | live.com | Email | Default |
| Accelerators | Map | | | |
| Tracking Protection | Map with Bing | bing.com | Map | Default |
| | Translate | | | |
| | Translate with Bing | microsofttranslator.com | Translate | Default |

Manage Add-ons

View and manage your Internet Explorer add-ons

E-mail with Windows Live

| | | | |
|---|---|---|---|
| Status: | Default | Home page: | http://mail.live.com/ |
| Available on: | Document, Selection, Link | Installed from: | http://go.microsoft.com/fwlink/?LinkID=99193 |
| Category: | Email change | | |

Remove as default    Disable    Remove

Find More Accelerators...
Learn more about Accelerators    Close

**Figure 5-19**

**Figure 5-20**

To obtain more accelerators, click the Find More Accelerators link at the bottom of the dialog box. Internet Explorer opens a new window containing a list of accelerators you can install. When you no longer want to use an accelerator, you can choose to disable it (which lets you enable it again later) or remove it (which uninstalls the accelerator and requires that you download it again to use it). When you have multiple accelerators in the same category, you can choose to set one as the default.

## Setting up tracking protection

Interestingly enough, Internet Explorer comes with no tracking-protection add-ons installed. Your virus protection software will likely install tracking protection as well. In addition, you can click the Get a Tracking Protection List Online link to obtain a tracking protection list. After Internet Explorer displays a list of tracking-protection sites, click Add to add the site to your list. Figure 5-21 shows what your tracking protection list would look like if you chose to add TRUSTe.

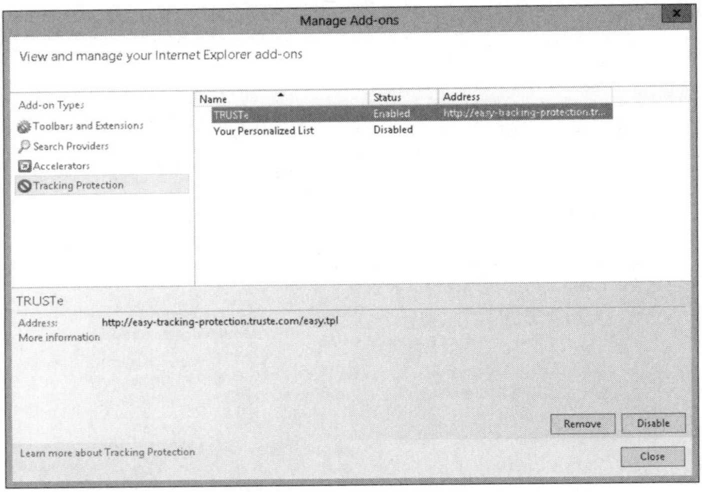

**Figure 5-21**

# *Using the Safety Features*

As threats to browsers have increased, so have the responses that browser vendors provide in the form of safety features. Internet Explorer contains a number of safety features to help make your browsing experience more secure. In some cases, such as deleting the browsing history, there's a trade-off between safety and functionality — you must choose one or the other.

Accessing the safety features is easy. Simply click Tools and choose an option from the Safety menu.

The following sections describe the various safety features that Internet Explorer provides and explains how to use them. In addition, many sections describe trade-offs that the safety feature presents and specify when it's more important to rely on the safety feature than to choose functionality.

## Deleting the browsing history

Removing your browsing history from a system prevents others from discovering where you've gone and what you've done while browsing. Removing your history from a home system may not be essential, but removing it from any public system you use *is* essential. Someone can learn a lot about you by simply checking where you've browsed during a session. Follow these steps to delete your browsing history:

*1.* **Choose Tools⇨Safety⇨Delete Browsing History or press Ctrl+Shift+Delete.**

Internet Explorer displays the Delete Browsing History dialog box. (See Figure 5-22.)

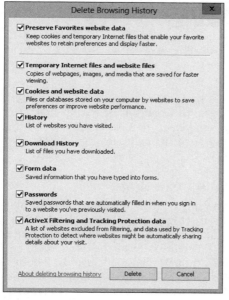

**Figure 5-22**

*2.* **Select the items you want to delete and clear the items you want to retain.**

*3.* **Click Delete.**

Internet Explorer removes all the items you selected from the browsing history.

## Finding out the web page privacy policy

The web page *privacy policy* tells you how a site is tracking and using your data. It's important to know this information because many sites simply assume that you've granted them permission to use your information in any way they deem fit. To see a site's privacy policy, choose Tools⇨Safety⇨Webpage Privacy Policy. You see its Privacy Report, like the one shown in Figure 5-23.

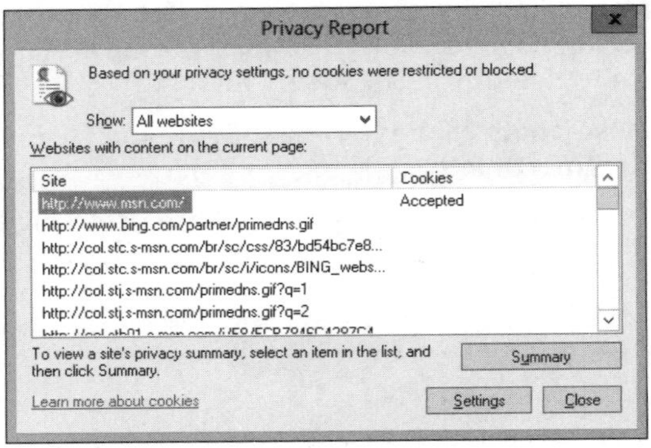

Privacy Report

Based on your privacy settings, no cookies were restricted or blocked.

Show: All websites

Websites with content on the current page:

| Site | Cookies |
| --- | --- |
| http://www.msn.com/ | Accepted |
| http://www.bing.com/partner/primedns.gif | |
| http://col.stc.s-msn.com/br/sc/css/83/bd54bc7e8... | |
| http://col.stc.s-msn.com/br/sc/i/icons/BING_webs... | |
| http://col.stj.s-msn.com/primedns.gif?q=1 | |
| http://col.stj.s-msn.com/primedns.gif?q=2 | |

To view a site's privacy summary, select an item in the list, and then click Summary.

Summary

Learn more about cookies

Settings    Close

**Figure 5-23**

This report shows that you're accepting cookies from only one of the URLs listed on this page. To see what that site does with the information, you select the URL in the list and then click Summary. You see the Privacy Policy dialog box, like the one shown in Figure 5-24.

## Using InPrivate browsing

The *InPrivate* browsing feature automatically disables many of the features in Internet Explorer. Choose Tools⇨Safety⇨ InPrivate Browsing to open a special Internet Explorer window. This window has InPrivate browsing enabled, and most of the activities you perform in it can't be tracked. Of course, this feature also disables your accelerators, toolbars, extensions, and other extended functionality. To ensure privacy, you work without the extras you normally use.

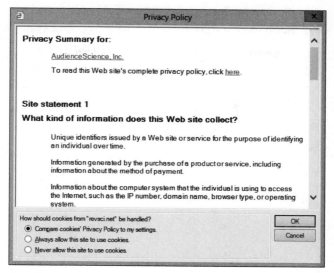

**Figure 5-24**

# Utilizing ActiveX Filtering

*ActiveX* controls are powerful add-ins for Internet Explorer (an *add-on* provides functionality on top of, but separately from Internet Explorer, while an *add-in* is made part of the Internet Explorer application environment). Many site designers use them to offer specific viewing experiences or to extend Internet Explorer's functionality in special ways. After you install an ActiveX control, any site that uses the control can access it. However, when you enable ActiveX Filtering by choosing Tools➪Safety➪ActiveX Filtering, Internet Explorer asks your permission before it allows a site to use an ActiveX control. Even if you choose to allow the site to use the control, you're at least aware that the control is in use. This feature makes you more aware of how sites are interacting with your system.

## Working with the SmartScreen Filter

The *SmartScreen Filter* helps you detect sites that are trying to install malware on your system (such as a virus) or carry out phishing attacks (such as gaining access to your Social Security number). The SmartScreen Filter automatically alerts you when it detects sites that are known to cause problems. However, it doesn't necessarily detect every potentially problematic site, because new sites appear every day. The following sections describe how you can locate and report problem sites.

### Checking a web page for potential problems

To check a site for potential problems, choose Tools⇨ Safety⇨Check This Website. You see the SmartScreen Filter dialog box, which tells you that Internet Explorer will send the URL of this site to Microsoft for checking. Click OK. After a few seconds, SmartScreen Filter returns with a report about whether the site contains dangerous elements.

### Reporting an unsafe web site to Microsoft

When you find a site that you think is dangerous, you can report it to Microsoft. Choose Tools⇨Safety⇨Report Unsafe Website. You see a new Internet Explorer window open to a page that contains a report form. Fill out the form and click Submit to send it to Microsoft.

# Configuring Your System

When you initially install Windows, what you receive is
Microsoft's best guess about how you want your system configured. Microsoft can make a lot of good guesses, but you'll
almost certainly want to change parts of the system configuration to appear as you want them to appear. In fact, if you've
read previous parts of this book, you've probably made a few
configuration changes already. This part helps you understand
the most common types of changes that people make to their
Windows installations. This part isn't a comprehensive look,
but you'll likely find that it can answer most (if not all) of your
configuration questions.

## In this part . . .

- Personalizing a Theme
- Accessing the Control Panel
- Choosing a Power Usage Plan
- Interacting with Device Manager
- Setting Up System Protection

# *Personalizing a Theme*

A *theme* defines the overall feel of your Windows setup. You define the colors your system uses, the sounds it plays to signal specific events, and the way it reacts when you leave it alone for too long (by setting the screen saver). Themes are important because they describe how you want Windows to "feel" as you use it. The following sections describe the theme options that users change most often.

## Adding a Desktop background

The *Desktop* is where you place all your applications and folders and other items you use to work. Choosing a new background for the Desktop makes your work environment friendlier. You can even tell Windows to automatically change the background for you so that it doesn't become boring. Microsoft provides a wealth of background options in Windows 8, or you can provide your own options. The following steps help you configure the Desktop background:

1. **Right-click the Desktop and choose Personalize from the context menu.**

   You see the Personalization window, as shown in Figure 6-1.

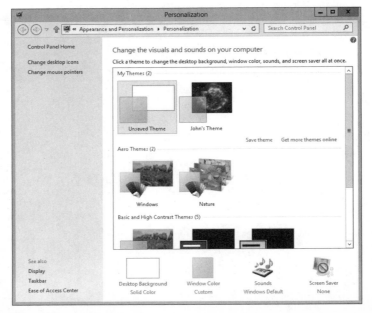

**Figure 6-1**

2. **Click Desktop Background at the bottom of the window.**

   You see the Desktop Background window. (See Figure 6-2.)

3. **Choose an option from the Picture Location drop-down list.**

   The Desktop Background window content changes to match the location you select. You can choose from these options:

   - **Windows Desktop Backgrounds:** Pictures that Microsoft provides as part of the Windows installation

   - **Pictures Library:** The images that appear in your My Pictures folder or as part of the Public Pictures folder

   - **Top Rated Photos:** Photographs that Microsoft provides as part of the Windows installation

   - **Solid Colors:** A single color that fills the entire Desktop area

   - **Desktop Background:** Any pictures that appear as part of a theme that you either create or install

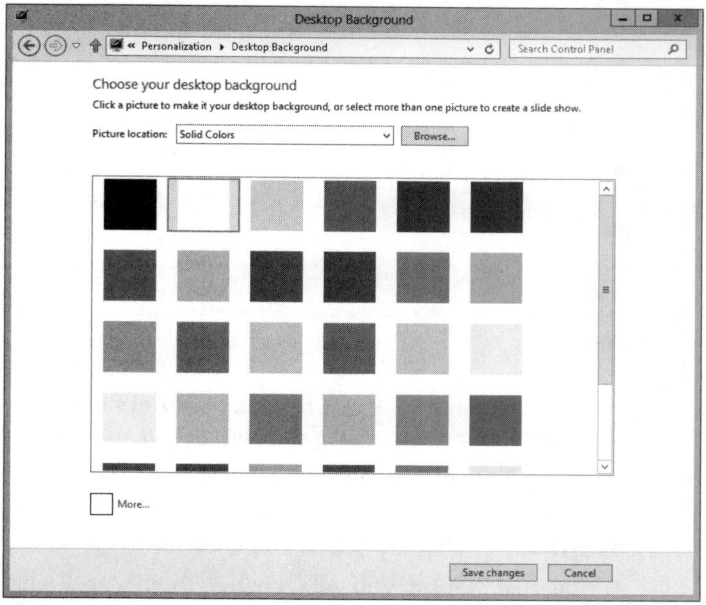

**Figure 6-2**

4. **(Optional) Select display options for the picture location you choose.**

   Each Desktop source provides a number of configuration options. For example, when working with solid colors, you can create custom colors to use in place of the defaults that Microsoft provides. When working with pictures, you can select the check boxes that appear next to every picture to select pictures for viewing. You can then tell Windows to change the picture at regular intervals. It's also possible to choose how Windows positions the picture, as shown in Figure 6-3.

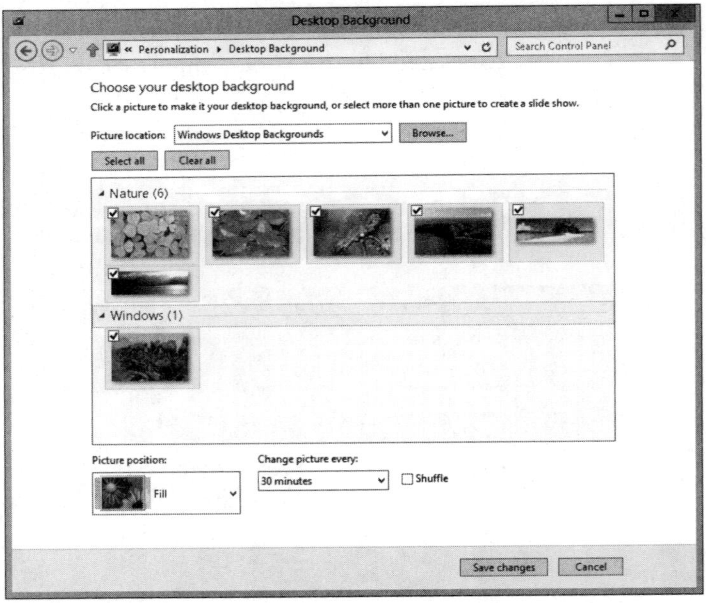

**Figure 6-3**

5. **Click Save Changes to make your changes permanent and then close the Personalization window.**

   Windows displays the changes you made to the Desktop.

## Adjusting the system colors

During installation, you get a chance to choose a color scheme for your Windows installation. The color scheme affects the *system colors* — the colors used by Windows and any application

that supports the use of system colors for displaying information. You may decide later that the color scheme you chose
when installing Windows doesn't meet your needs. Perhaps you
can't see the colors well enough in the lighting conditions in
your office, or you may find that you need different colors in
different settings.

An application developer can always choose to use custom
colors in an application, which means that it ignores the system
colors provided by Windows. In most cases, these applications
let you choose colors as part of the application configuration,
so you need to skim the documentation that comes with the
application for setup instructions. The following steps help you
modify the color settings used for Windows and any applications that rely on the system color settings:

*1.* **Right-click the Desktop and choose Personalize from
    the context menu.**

    You see the Personalization window.

*2.* **Click Window Color at the bottom of the window.**

    You see the Window Color and Appearance window, as
    shown in Figure 6-4.

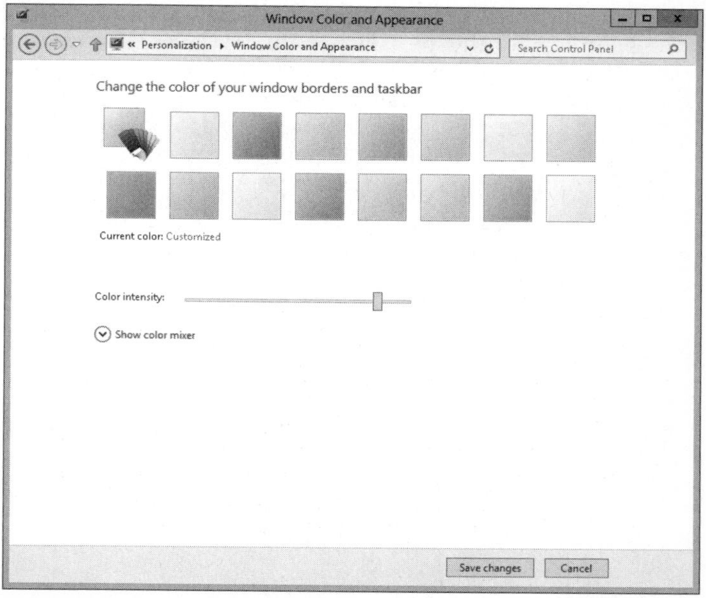

| | Window Color and Appearance | | ─ □ ✕ |
|---|---|---|---|
| ← → ⌄ ⬆ « Personalization ▸ Window Color and Appearance | | ⌄ ↻ | Search Control Panel 🔎 |

Change the color of your window borders and taskbar

Current color: Customized

Color intensity: ▐

⌄ Show color mixer

Save changes    Cancel

**Figure 6-4**

3. **Select the color block that looks closest to the color you want to use for your display.**

   You see the color of the window border change in response to your selections. This change helps you determine whether the new color will meet your needs.

4. **Fine-tune the color selection by moving the Color Intensity slider as needed.**

   The color becomes lighter as you move the slider to the left, and darker as you move the slider to the right.

5. **Click Save Changes to make your changes permanent, and then close the Personalization window.**

   Windows displays the changes you made to any applications you have open.

You may decide that you don't like any predefined colors that Microsoft provides. To create a custom color, click Show Color Mixer. You see three sliders that control the amount of red, green, and blue the display uses. Use these sliders to create a custom color for your windows.

## Calibrating your monitor for optimal appearance

Monitors are normally shipped from the factory with optimal settings for the average person. However, few average persons live on the planet, and none of us views color in precisely the same way. As a consequence, you need to tune your monitor so that you see colors as they're meant to be seen from your perspective. The following steps help you calibrate your monitor for optimal appearance from your perspective:

1. **Right-click the Desktop and choose Personalize from the context menu.**

   You see the Personalization window.

2. **Click Display on the left side of the window.**

   You see the Display window, as shown in Figure 6-5.

3. **Click Calibrate Color on the left side of the window.**

   The Display Color Calibration Wizard starts. Be sure to read the instructions you see on each screen because they help you get the most out of your particular monitor.

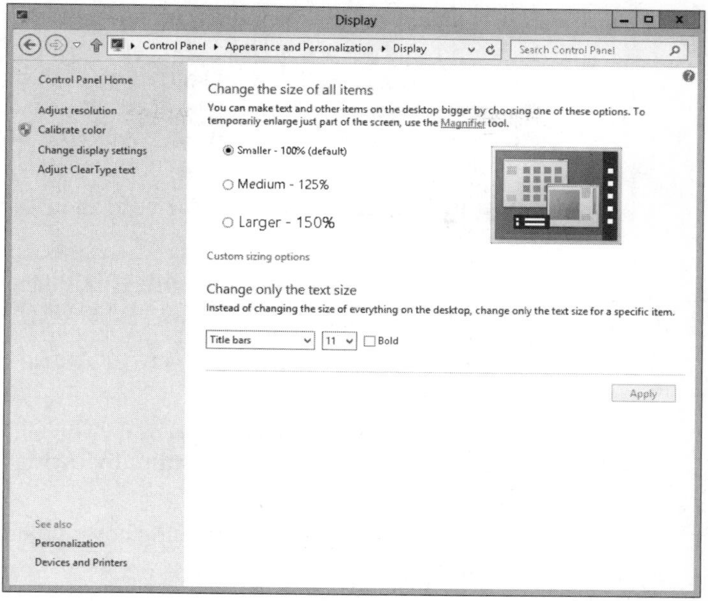

**Figure 6-5**

4. **Click Next.**

   You see instructions telling you to verify the capabilities of your monitor before you begin this process. The most important item to know is the location of the Menu button on your monitor. The Menu button provides access to the various features that your monitor provides, such as adjusting brightness, contrast, and colors.

5. **Click Next.**

   The wizard tells you how to set the gamma correction on your monitor. The fancy term *gamma* describes a mathematical relationship between colors used to display content on your monitor. All you really need to know is that you want balanced color so that you can see every color equally well.

6. **Click Next.**

   You see a screen with a slider that lets you adjust the gamma correction on your monitor. What you want to do is match the big picture on this screen to the middle picture on the previous screen.

Click the Back button located in the upper-left corner of the window as needed so that you can see the previous page of the wizard. Click Next so that you can make adjustments as needed. Most of these adjustments require that you move back and forth between pages so that you can compare your display with the sample pictures provided.

7. **Adjust the gamma correction for your monitor and then click Next.**

You see instructions for setting the brightness and contrast of your monitor. What the instructions don't tell you is that these settings interact. You need to go back and forth between the four pages to adjust for any interaction.

8. **Use the four pages of brightness and contrast adjustment to set your monitor for optimal viewing and then click Next.**

You see the instructions for making color balance changes.

9. **Click Next.**

You see a page with three color sliders for adjusting the display's color balance.

A common mistake is to set the gamma correction incorrectly, in which case you'll find that you never see the X behind the man when making the brightness adjustment. If you fail to see the X, no matter how bright your display becomes, the gamma correction is set too low. Adjust the gamma correction again (even if it doesn't quite match the picture) and try setting the brightness again.

10. **Use the three color sliders to adjust the color balance of the display, and then click Next.**

The wizard asks you to check the calibration. Click Current Calibration to see the adjustments you've made. Click Previous Calibration to see the original setup of your system.

11. **Click Finish to complete the wizard.**

You see the adjustments you've made to your monitor's setup. If you selected the option Start ClearType Tuner When I Click Finish to Ensure that Text Appears Correctly, the ClearType Tuner Wizard starts. See the next section of this part for details.

12. **Close the Display window.**

You're ready to go back to work!

## Modifying ClearType

ClearType makes the text on your display look clear when you're using a liquid crystal display (LCD), such as one that comes with a laptop system. You don't use ClearType when working with an older cathode ray tube (CRT) that comes with certain desktop systems (although most desktops now use LCDs as well). Adjusting ClearType after you adjust the display settings can help you get more out of this technology and reduce eyestrain, which can lead to headaches and other physical problems. The following steps describe how to tune ClearType:

1. **Right-click the Desktop and choose Personalize from the context menu.**

   You see the Personalization window.

2. **Click Display on the left side of the window.**

   You see the Display window.

3. **Click Adjust ClearType Text on the left side of the window.**

   You see the ClearType Text Tuner Wizard. (See Figure 6-6.) Notice the Turn On ClearType check box. If you don't have ClearType turned on, you can't make the adjustments in the remaining steps.

4. **Select Turn On ClearType and then click Next.**

   If your monitor isn't set to its *native* resolution (the resolution at which the monitor works best), you see a display asking whether you want to change the resolution to the native resolution. ClearType always works best at a monitor's native resolution. However, you may need the monitor set to another resolution for specific purposes. Set the monitor to the resolution you use most often and adjust ClearType for that resolution.

5. **Select either the current resolution or the native resolution, and click Next.**

   You see the first of five sample text screens.

**Figure 6-6**

6. **Choose the sample that looks best to you and then click Next.**

   You see another sample text screen.

7. **Repeat Step 6 for each of the five sample text screens.**

8. **Click Finish to complete the wizard.**

   You see the results of your adjustments onscreen.

## Setting up system sounds

People associate specific sounds with particular events. When a cellphone rings with a particular ringtone, you know that it's Aunt Martha calling. The sounds that Microsoft provides with Windows are designed to work in an office environment — they're intended to provide subtle sounds that don't disturb anyone. If you have a home office, you might decide that you want a bit more pizzazz. The following steps tell how to change your system sounds:

1. **Right-click the Desktop and choose Personalize from the context menu.**

   You see the Personalization window.

2. **Click Sounds at the bottom of the window.**

You see the Sounds tab of the Sound dialog box, as shown in Figure 6-7.

3. **Select an event that you want to modify.**

Windows provides a lot of different events. For example, you can assign a sound to the default beep or to dialog boxes that contain the exclamation mark. Browsing the event list may give you all sorts of ideas for customizing your setup.

4. **Select a sound to associate with the event from the Sounds drop-down list box.**

The Sounds list box contains the default Windows sounds. You can also click Browse to locate and use custom sounds with your system.

5. **Click Test to listen to the sound.**

Always make sure that the sound works as you anticipate.

6. **Perform Steps 3 through 5 for each event you want to modify.**

7. **Click OK.**

Windows begins using the sounds you selected.

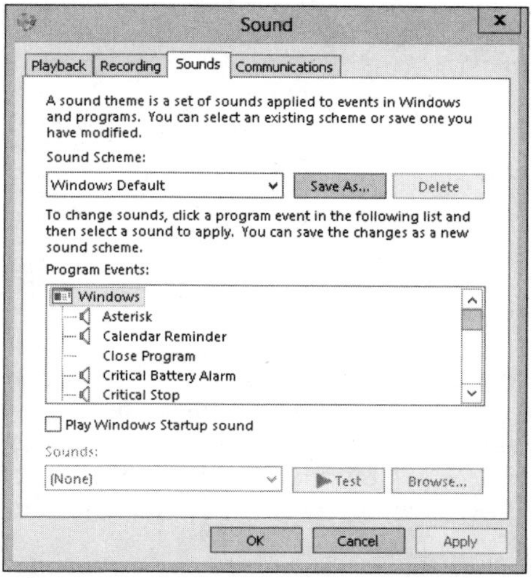

**Figure 6-7**

# *Accessing the Control Panel*

The Control Panel provides access to a number of *applets*, which are special applications used to configure specific parts of your system. For example, the Language applet helps you configure your system to use more than one language or a different language from the one installed by default. Use these steps to open the Control Panel:

1. **Press Win+C.**

   You see the Charms bar.

2. **Click the Settings charm.**

   You see the Settings page.

3. **Click Control Panel.**

   You see the Control Panel window as shown in Figure 6-8.

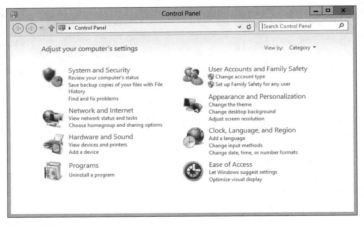

**Figure 6-8**

The Category view of the Control Panel that you see consists of major categories and subcategories. Click a link to access that Control Panel feature. You can also change the view to Large Icons or to Small Icons using the View By drop-down list. The icon view works best when you know the name of the applet you want to use.

The following sections describe some of the applets you use most often to configure the system. (You can find other applets described in other parts of this book, such as the Power Options applet described in the "Choosing a Power Usage Plan" section, later in this part.)

## Turning Windows 8 features on or off

Installing third-party applications usually consists of putting a disk in a drive and waiting for the application installation process to start. When working with Windows 8 apps, you go to the store and obtain the app you want to use, as described in The Big Picture. Windows 8 also comes with features that are installed, but turned off by default. To use these features, you must turn them on. The following steps describe how to perform this task:

*1.* **Open the Control Panel and click the Programs category.**

You see a list of program-related links. (See Figure 6-9.)

**Figure 6-9**

*2.* **Click Turn Windows Features On or Off in the Programs and Features group.**

You see the Windows Features dialog box, as shown in Figure 6-10.

**Figure 6-10**

3. **Select any features you want to turn on and clear the check box next to any features you want to turn off.**

When you're not quite sure what task a particular feature performs, hover the mouse over the feature and you'll see a Help balloon that provides a short description of the feature. In many cases, the Help balloon provides enough information to help you make an informed decision about turning the feature on or off.

4. **Click OK.**

Windows turns the required features on or off as you requested.

## Making your system more accessible

Some Control Panel applets are actually mini-applications. Yes, they eventually end up adjusting settings, but you'll see them more as wizards. For example, when you click Let Windows Suggest Settings in the Ease of Access group of the Control Panel, you see a wizard that asks questions about how you interact with the computer, as shown in Figure 6-11.

This wizard is helpful even if you have problems using the computer that aren't normally considered special needs, such as blindness. Simply answer each question that the wizard asks and you'll eventually see suggestions for making Windows easier to work with from a human interaction perspective.

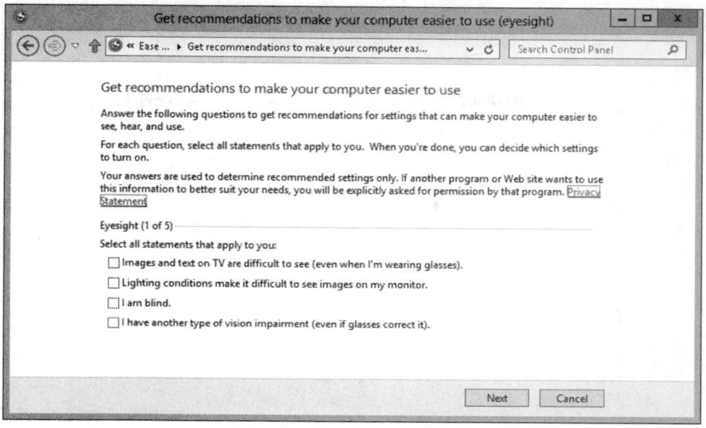

**Figure 6-11**

## Modifying the default programs

Windows provides the means to adjust a number of default settings. For example, you can adjust how Windows reacts to certain types of media. It's also possible to select the default application used to open a particular file extension. One of the most common defaults to manage, however, is the default program used for a particular task. The following steps tell you how to configure a default program:

*1.* **Open the Control Panel and click the Programs category.**

You see a list of program-related links.

*2.* **Click Set Your Default Programs in the Default Programs group.**

You see the Set Default Programs window, as shown in Figure 6-12. Notice the list of programs along the left side of the window. Selecting a particular program lets you modify its defaults.

*3.* **Click Set This Program As Default when you want the program to open, by default, every file type and protocol that it can. Otherwise, click Choose Defaults for This Program.**

When you click Choose Defaults for This Program, you see the Set Program Associations window, such as the one in Figure 6-13, where you choose which files and protocols are associated with the program:

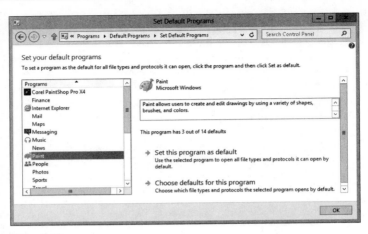

**Figure 6-12**

**Figure 6-13**

> a. *Place a check mark next to each file extension or proto-col that you want to associate with the application.*
>
> b. *Click Save.*
>
> Windows saves the associations you've created for that particular program.

4. **Repeat Step 3 for each of the programs you want to modify.**

5. **Click OK to close the Set Default Programs window, and then close the Default Programs window.**

    Windows begins using the defaults you've created.

# Choosing a Power Usage Plan

Just about everyone is concerned about power usage today because every electron they use translates into money spent. Of course, you also have to be able to access your system in order to perform useful tasks. When a system shuts down components too quickly or runs at half-speed most of the time, you can't accomplish as much useful work. Consequently, there's a trade-off between the power usage required to perform useful work and the power savings needed to conserve resources. That's where a power usage plan comes into play. The following steps describe how to choose a power usage plan for your system:

*1.* **Open the Control Panel and click the Hardware and Sound category.**

    You see a list of hardware-related and sound-related links. (See Figure 6-14.)

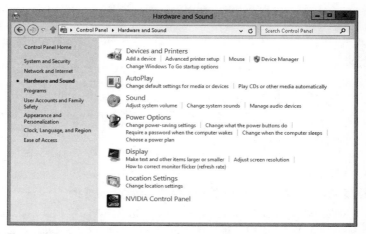

**Figure 6-14**

2. **Click Choose a Power Plan in the Power Options group.**

   You see a list of the standard power usage options provided with Windows, as shown in Figure 6-15.

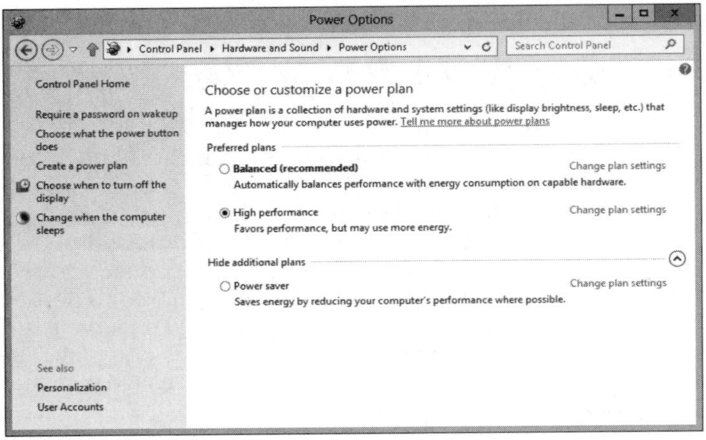

**Figure 6-15**

3. **Choose the power plan you want to use and close the Power Options window.**

   Windows uses the power plan you selected when managing power on the system.

   The default power plans provide significant flexibility in managing the power resources on your system. Simply click Change Plan Settings to change the features for a particular plan. For example, you may choose a longer interval before Windows automatically shuts down the display after a period of nonusage. Longer intervals cause the system to use more power.

# Interacting with Device Manager

Every device on your system requires access to system resources. A device obtains this access through a *device driver* that requests the required resources from Windows. In addition, devices can provide configuration utilities that help you change how the device operates. For example, you can configure a monitor to present information in portrait view rather than in the standard landscape view. The process of obtaining access to resources and changing the way the device works is called *device management,* and the Device Manager provides the required access to these settings.

Device Manager can also alert you to hardware-related problems. Many hardware failures are obvious. For example, when the audio system isn't functioning, you don't hear sounds coming from the speaker. Some hardware failures hide, though, and cause less conspicuous problems. Installing a standard VBA driver for your high–end graphics adapter still allows Windows to display images onscreen, but without the benefits that the high-end graphics adapter provides. As a result, your system works slower than if it had the correct driver installed. Viewing the status of devices in Device Manager is an important part of maintaining your system. The following steps provide a quick process for viewing and fixing simple errors with your hardware:

1. **Open the Control Panel and click the Hardware and Sound category.**

   You see a list of hardware-related and sound-related links.

2. **Click the Device Manager link in the Devices and Printers group.**

   You see the Device Manager window, as shown in Figure 6-16. Notice that every device appears within a group. For example, all drives appear in the Disk Drives group.

   Windows tells you when it detects a problem with a particular device. Notice that the SM Bus Controller entry in Figure 6-16 has a yellow icon on it. This icon is a triangle with an exclamation mark in it. When you see this icon, you know that the device is *banged* — it's nonfunctional.

3. **Right-click any banged devices in the list and choose Update Driver Software from the context menu.**

   Windows starts the Update Driver Software Wizard.

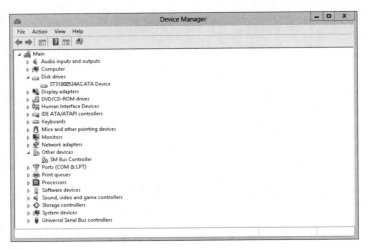

**Figure 6-16**

4. **Click Search Automatically for Updated Driver Software.**

   Windows searches the local drives and online for a driver for the device. If Windows finds one, it automatically installs the device driver for you. In some cases, you must contact the vendor to obtain an appropriate driver for the device. In this case, you choose the Browse My Computer for Driver Software option and tell Windows where to find the driver you obtained from the vendor.

5. **Perform Steps 3 and 4 for all banged devices on your system.**

6. **Repeat Steps 3 and 4 for any device that's incorrectly identified on your system.**

   Look for devices that have generic names, such as VGA graphics, rather than specific names, like NVIDIA GeForce GTX 580.

7. **Close the Device Manager window.**

   Windows normally begins using the updated device drivers immediately. In some cases, you must restart the system to obtain full use of the device drivers and their associated software.

# *Setting Up System Protection*

The focus of all computer systems is the data that they maintain and manage. The purpose of the software and hardware is to make it easy for you to manage information in a number of ways. Without data, a computer system is useless, even if everything else about it is intact. It should come as no surprise then that protecting the data on a computer becomes an essential task. Even if the rest of the system becomes nonfunctional, you can always obtain new applications and hardware, and become fully functional again, as long as your data remain safe. The following sections describe one level of data protection — the use of restore points to keep your system from being damaged by updates.

## Accessing the restore points

One of the most common issues that arise is the damage done by a system update. Every time you perform a system update of any kind, you take the risk that the update will cause damage to the system as a whole and to the data that the system manages. Windows provides a method to set aside part of your hard drive as a location for information used to restore the drive later if damage occurs. This information is the *restore point*. However, before you can use restore points, you must tell Windows to protect the drive and to set aside a certain amount of space on it for restoration information. The following steps tell you how to access the restore point information on your system:

1.  **Open the Control Panel and click the System and Security category.**

    You see a list of system-related and security-related links, as shown in Figure 6-17.

2.  **Click the System group link.**

    You see the System window. (See Figure 6-18.)

**Figure 6-17**

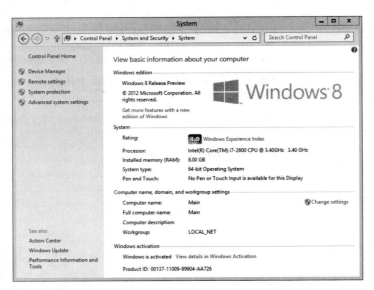

**Figure 6-18**

**3. Click System Protection on the left side of the window.**

You see the System Protection tab of the System Properties dialog box. (See Figure 6-19.) This tab contains all the functionality needed to protect your system using restore points. You can also determine the status of each drive on the system. In this case, drive D has no protection, but drive C does have protection.

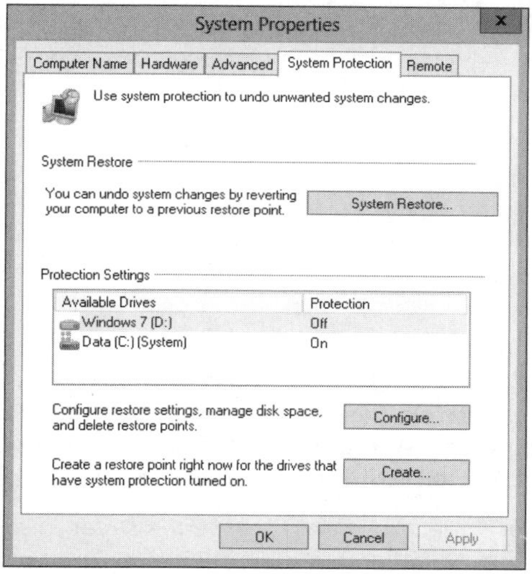

**Figure 6-19**

## Choosing drives to protect

After you open the System Protection tab of the System Properties dialog box, you can begin working with restore points. The first task is to tell Windows which drives to protect with a restore point. The system drive — the one used to boot the system and hold the Windows files — is always protected by default. However, you may also want to protect important data drives. Use these steps to change the protection status of a drive:

**1. Select the drive you want to protect in the list provided in the dialog box.**

**2. Click Configure.**

You see the System Protection dialog box, like the one shown in Figure 6-20. (Each drive has its own protection.)

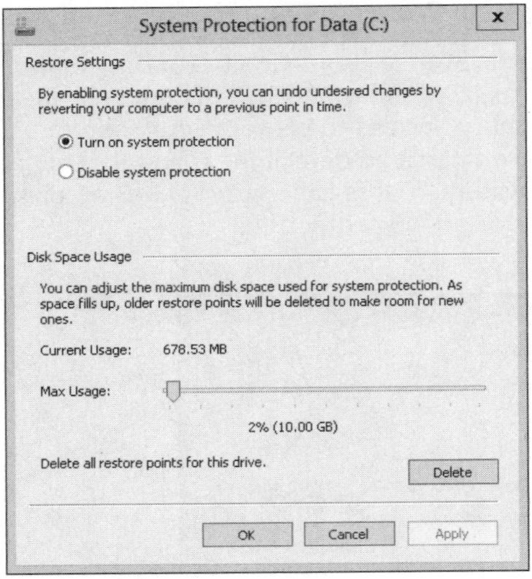

**Figure 6-20**

3. **Select Turn On System Protection to use restore points or select Disable System Protection to stop using restore points. When turning on system protection, follow these additional configuration steps:**

   - *When protecting a drive, move the slider to select the amount of disk space used to hold restore points.*

     The default setting uses 10GB for system restore points, which is more than sufficient in most cases — use more space when you want a longer restore point history.

   - *When disabling the use of restore points, click Delete to remove the restore point data from the drive.*

4. **Click OK.**

   Windows modifies the restore point support for the drive as you configured it.

## Creating a restore point

The act of creating a restore point saves data about the drive so that the drive can be restored later if it becomes damaged in some way from an application or update. Restore points act as one level of system restoration — one that's easy and quick to maintain.

Restore points don't serve the same purpose as backups. The drive hardware must remain in good shape to use a restore point. If your drive hardware fails, you must use a backup to restore the data to your new hard drive. Likewise, restore points don't protect your data from user actions, such as accidental file deletion. Use these steps to create a restore point:

1. **Click Create.**

   You see the System Protection dialog box. It asks you to provide a description of the restore point.

2. **Type a short description of the restore point, such as why you made it.**

   Windows automatically provides information, such as the restore point date, as part of the restore point.

3. **Click Create.**

   Windows temporarily displays a dialog box telling you that it's creating the restore point. When the restore point is finished, Windows displays another dialog box.

4. **Click Close.**

   The restore point is ready for use later.

## Reverting to a restore point

When damage occurs, you can use a restore point to restore the data on the hard drive, assuming that the drive hardware remains intact. Use these steps to restore a drive from a restore point:

1. **Click System Restore.**

   You see the System Restore Wizard start.

2. **Click Next.**

   The wizard displays a list of restore points for the system, as shown in Figure 6-21. Notice that the restore points include a description, the date the restore point was created, and how the restore point was made. (Any restore points you create are classified as *manual* restore points.)

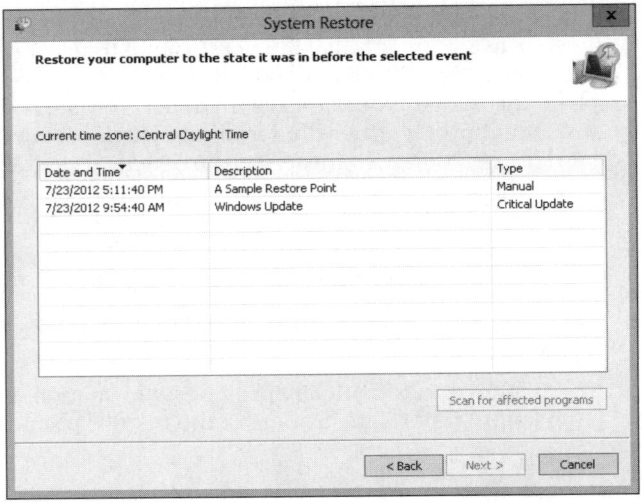

**Figure 6-21**

3.  **Select the restore point you want to use and click Next.**

    The wizard displays a summary screen that shows which tasks it will perform.

4.  **Click Finish.**

    The wizard restores your system. You may be asked to reboot the system when this process is complete.

# Interacting with External Devices

Managing data is the focal point of every computer system. The computer hardware makes it possible to manipulate the data and applications to provide the user with an interface for interacting with both data and hardware. However, a successful computer system normally needs something more, in the form of external devices, for input and output. Cameras, scanners, and other such devices provide input for the computer, and printers and faxes provide output. This part can't provide a complete view of interacting with external devices, but it does provide you with a good overview of the external devices most commonly used to enhance the input and output capabilities of a computer system.

## In this part . . .

- ✔ Adding Device Support
- ✔ Configuring a Printer
- ✔ Controlling Print Jobs
- ✔ Setting Up a Scanner
- ✔ Scanning a Document
- ✔ Working with Pictures

# Adding Device Support

In most cases, when you connect any device to your system, Windows automatically detects the device and begins installing support for it. The device must be active. In other words, it has to have power applied to it and be ready to use. When Windows successfully detects the device, you see the Device Setup dialog box, like the one shown in Figure 7-1.

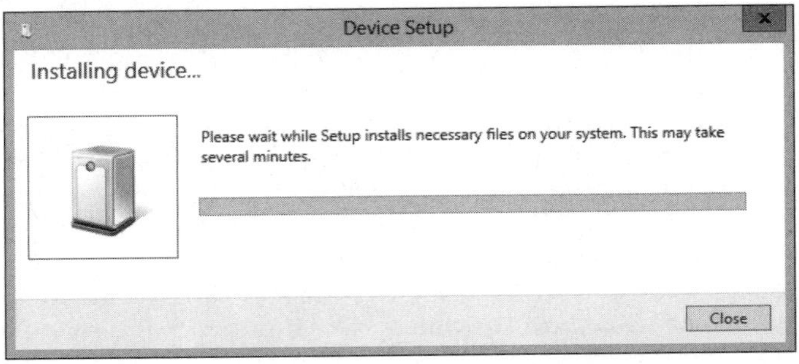

**Device Setup** ✕

Installing device...

Please wait while Setup installs necessary files on your system. This may take several minutes.

Close

**Figure 7-1**

The support you get from Windows is generic in this case. Yes, you can access the device, but Microsoft doesn't install any special utilities that come with the device. In addition, the device may work better (by working faster or providing special functionality) when using vendor-supplied drivers. However, you need a Windows 8 support disc for the device. Windows 7 (and older) support appears to have some issues when working on Windows 8, so using the generic drivers that come with automatic detection are probably the best bet in many situations.

After the driver installation is complete, you can check for the device in the Control Panel. Printers, scanners, cameras, and many other devices appear in the Devices and Printers window. To access this window, click the View Devices and Printers link in the Hardware and Sound group of the Control Panel. Figure 7-2 shows a typical view of that window. (Your window will look different unless you have installed precisely the same devices as I have.)

When you select any device, Windows provides status information about it at the bottom of the window. For example, when selecting the HP Officejet 5600 Series entry, you can see that this is a multifunction device — it provides printer, scanner, and copying services. In addition, this is the *default device* — the one that Windows uses unless you specify that you want to use a different device for printing or scanning in a particular situation. It's important to set the default device by right-clicking the device you use most often and choosing Set As Default from the context menu.

Pay special attention to the Status field after installing a new device. Windows doesn't tell you that you have to restart the system to use the device. However, the Status field tells you that the device is inaccessible in this case until you restart the system. Checking the device status reduces unexplained problems in using the device later.

**Figure 7-2**

# Configuring a Printer

Printers offer several levels of configuration. In fact, depending on your printer, you can easily get lost in the vast array of settings that probably won't help much in day-to-day printing tasks. In most cases, all you really need to do is set up the type of paper, the orientation of the printout, and the quality of the print. The following steps tell how to perform this task:

*1.* **Click the View Devices and Printers link in the Hardware and Sound group of the Control Panel.**

You see the Devices and Printers window, containing a list of the devices and printers installed on your machine.

2.  **Right-click the device you want to configure and choose Printing Preferences from the context menu.**

    Windows displays the Printing Preferences dialog box, similar to the one shown in Figure 7-3. (Every printer vendor supplies a somewhat different dialog box, and every printer also has different capabilities, so your display won't precisely match this one.)

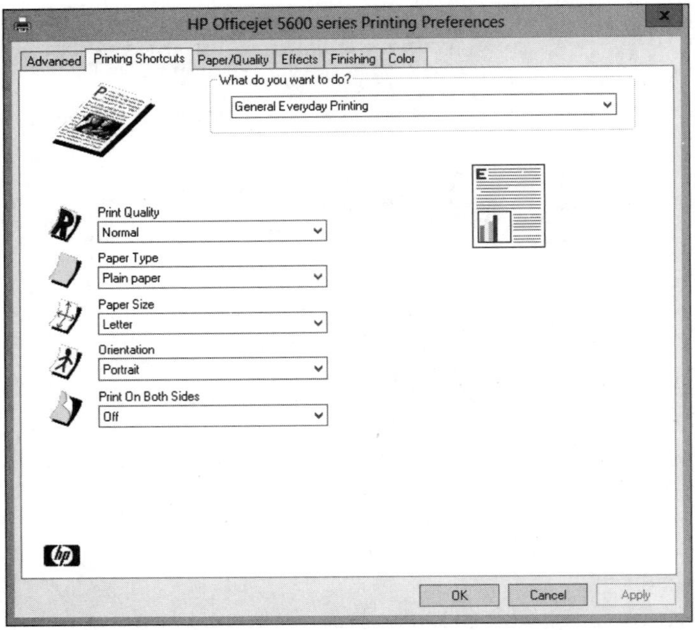

**Figure 7-3**

3.  **Select a default configuration from the What Do You Want to Do? list box, or configure the individual settings as needed.**

4.  **Click OK.**

    Windows configures the printer to use the new settings by default when printing a document.

# *Controlling Print Jobs*

In most cases, you send a print job to the printer, wait for a while, and then pick up the results. However, in some situations you have a large number of print jobs to send to the printer or you have especially complex jobs that require some level of management. The following sections discuss the most common management tasks and tell you how to perform them.

## Accessing the list of print jobs

Whenever you print a document, Windows places a printer icon in the Notification Area. Windows removes the printer icon automatically when the print jobs sent to the printer are complete. To see the list of jobs that the printer is working on, double-click the printer icon in the Notification Area. You see a status window like the one shown in Figure 7-4.

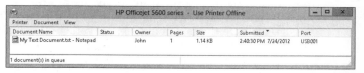

| Document Name | Status | Owner | Pages | Size | Submitted | Port |
|---|---|---|---|---|---|---|
| My Text Document.txt - Notepad | | John | 1 | 1.14 KB | 2:40:30 PM 7/24/2012 | USB001 |

1 document(s) in queue

**Figure 7-4**

The top of the window tells you the printer status. To capture the screen shot easily, I placed the printer in an offline state. Your printer is normally online. However, if you see that the printer is offline, check its status and determine why it's offline.

Each print job appears on a separate line. You see information such as the document name, the application that printed it, who printed the document, the number of pages, the size of the document, when it was submitted for printing, and the port used to print the document. In some cases, you also see status information for the print job, such as whether it has been paused.

You can always double-click a print job to see the Printing Preferences dialog box. This dialog box shows the print preferences used to print that document. If you decide that you need a different print setup, you can reconfigure the print options and click OK. As long as the print job hasn't started printing, Windows uses the new settings to print the document.

## Pausing a print job

When a printer jams or you see other problems (such as an empty printer tray) with a print job, you may need to pause the print job, correct the problem, and then resume the print job. Pausing the print job lets other print jobs complete while this particular print job waits for the correct conditions. A paused print job shows the Paused indicator in the Status field of the printer's status window.

Whenever you want to pause a print job, open the printer's status window, right-click the print job entry, and choose Pause from the context menu. The job's status indicator will change. After you correct any issue that prevents the print job from completing, you can resume the print job by right-clicking the print job's entry and choosing Resume from the context menu.

Sometimes, you pause a print job too late, and part of the job is ruined by whatever conditions caused it to print incorrectly. In these cases, right-click the print job in the printer's status window, and choose Restart from the context menu. The job starts over from the beginning so that you get the desired output without having to submit the job again.

## Altering print job priorities

Every print job you submit starts at the lowest priority. However, if your customer is sitting in the lounge, waiting for an important document, and another user has just submitted a huge report that will take hours to complete, the customer won't likely wait long. The solution is to give your job a higher priority and pause the current job. Windows always prints the highest-priority job first. Use these steps to change the printing priority:

1. **Double-click the print job.**

   You see the print job's Properties dialog box open.

2. **Click the General tab.**

   Windows displays general information about the print job, including the print job priority, as shown in Figure 7-5.

3. **Move the Priority slider to give the print job a higher priority.**

   The Properties dialog box shows the priority change.

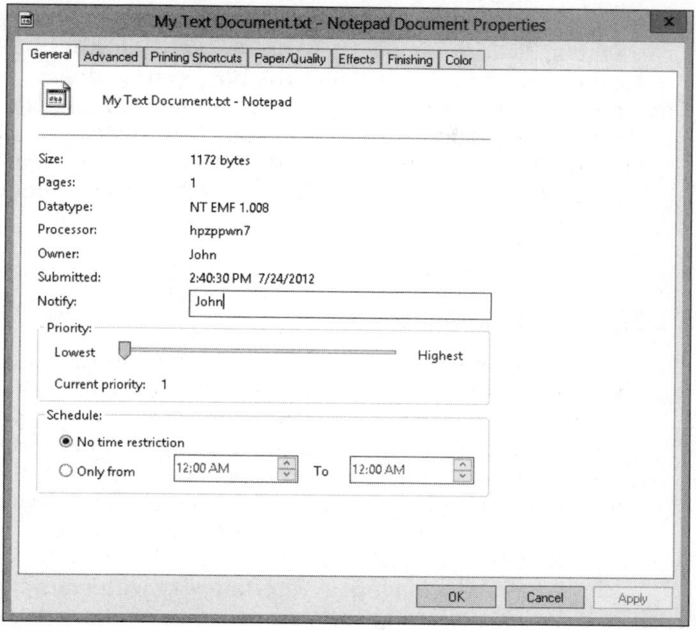

Figure 7-5

4. **Click OK.**

    The dialog box closes, and Windows assigns the print job a higher priority. When another print job has a higher priority, Windows still prints that job first. However, your print job prints before any lower-priority job in the queue. When two jobs have the same priority, Windows prints the job that was submitted first.

## Canceling a print job

Accidents can happen, and sometimes a print job is submitted by mistake. In this case, you can cancel the print job before it wastes a whole tree's worth of paper. To cancel a print job, you right-click its entry in the printer's status window and choose Cancel from the context menu. Windows asks whether you're sure that you want to cancel the print job. Click Yes to complete the task. The print job's entry disappears from the printer's status window.

There are situations where the print job will get stuck in a spooling loop, especially when printing to a remote system (such as a server with a printer attached). In most cases, you must cancel the print job on the server instead of the client system. Unfortunately, there are times when you simply can't cancel the print job because the host system doesn't respond. There doesn't seem to be any specific set of circumstances that cause this particular issue, and your only choice may be to physically shut the printer off, wait until the spooler recognizes that the printer is no longer available, and then cancel the print job.

# Setting Up a Scanner

Generally, you configure a scanner's characteristics, such as whether the flatbed or sheet feeder is the default, using the controls on the scanner's front panel. In rare cases, you can also configure them from your computer, but most vendors don't offer this option. However, you do need to configure the computer to perform the scan. You can perform this task manually every time you scan a document or you can create preset scanning policies, called *profiles*. A profile makes it fast and easy to scan documents in a certain way with consistent results. The following sections describe how to work with profiles to better your scanning experience.

## Checking the profiles

Before you can do anything with the scanner, you need to know which profiles are available. To see the profiles, right-click the scanner's entry in the Devices and Printers window and choose Scan Profiles from the context menu. You see the default scan profiles provided for your particular scanner, along with any new profiles you may have created, as shown in Figure 7-6.

Each entry tells you the associated scanner's name, the name of the profile, and the characteristics for that scan. The entries don't tell you the scan source, which is typically the flatbed scanner or the document feeder, depending on the capabilities of your scanner. You see the file output type for the scan, which can be bitmap (.BMP), Joint Pictures Experts Group (.JPG), Portable Network Graphic (.PNG), or Tagged Image Format (.TIF).

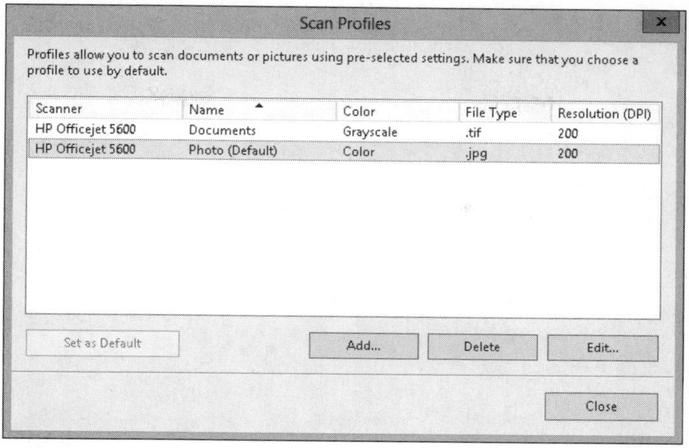

Figure 7-6

## Creating a new profile or editing an existing profile

It's possible to add new profiles or edit existing profiles as needed so that the settings reflect precisely what you need. For example, Windows assumes that you want a scan at 200 dots per inch (dpi). Most scanners provide much higher resolutions that produce better results when printed. You may decide to change the defaults to use a scan of 600 dpi instead. In some cases, you may need to scan sources that don't work well with the document feeder, or you may want to use the document feeder in situations where many people wouldn't use it. In short, you can add or edit profiles as needed using the following steps:

1. **When editing a profile, select the profile you want to change in the Scan Profiles window.**

2. **Click Add or Edit as needed.**

   You see either the Add New Profile or Edit Profile dialog box, as shown in Figure 7-7. (They look precisely the same except for the title.)

3. **Choose the appropriate scanner from the list.**

4. **When adding a new profile, type a profile name in the Profile Name field.**

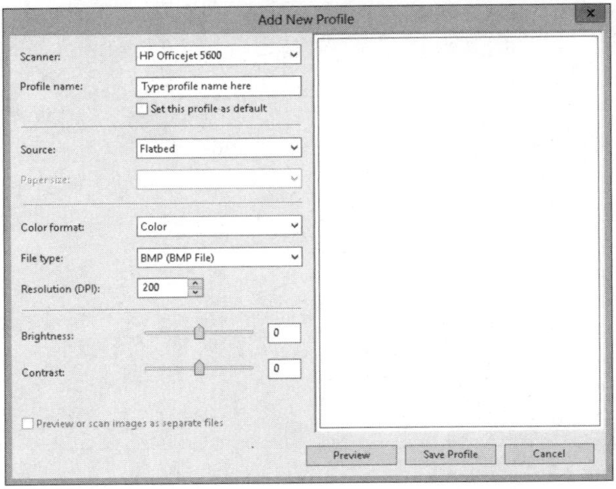

**Figure 7-7**

5. **Choose an option in the Source field.**

   The Flatbed option lets you scan images one at a time and tends to produce the most precise results because you place each item you want to scan on the scan surface individually. The Feeder option feeds one document at a time through the scanner and automates the task of scanning a lot of pages. When working with the document feeder, you must also provide a paper size.

6. **Choose a color format: Color, Grayscale, or Black and White.**

   Most people choose color for pictures and other graphics, grayscale for graphical text, and black-and-white for pure text. However, you may find that you want to scan some pictures in grayscale, rather than in color, to make them easier to configure for printing.

7. **Choose the output file type: BMP, JPG, PNG, or TIF.**

8. **Set the resolution in dpi.**

   The higher you set the dpi, the more accurately your scan reflects the original image. However, large dpi values also increase the size of the resulting file. Consequently, you often find that you must weigh the benefits of picture quality against the cost of large file sizes. (For example, large files generally use more ink or toner to print.)

*9.* **When working with the flatbed scanner, place in the scanner a typical image that you want to scan and then click Preview.**

Windows scans the object for you and displays the result in the preview area. When you're working with a document feeder, the preview option isn't available. You need to perform a test run and then make any required adjustments to obtain the best average results.

*10.* **If the output doesn't reflect the original, adjust the Brightness and Contrast controls as needed to obtain a better result.**

You may not be able to match colors precisely, but you can obtain a close approximation of the original, especially when working with text or grayscale images.

*11.* **Repeat Steps 9 and 10 until the output matches the original closely.**

*12.* **Click Save Profile.**

Windows creates the new profile for you.

## Establishing a profile as the default

Most people use the same type of scan most of the time. For example, if you regularly scan documents, you find that you use some sort of grayscale profile for the scans. To save time and effort — and reduce the potential for error — set the profile you use most often as the default. To perform this task, select the profile and click Set As Default in the Scan Profiles window.

## Removing a profile

When you find that you no longer need a profile, you can remove it from the list. Removing profiles you no longer need minimizes clutter and makes it easier for you to select the right profile from the list. To delete an existing profile, select the profile and click Delete in the Scan Profiles window.

# Scanning a Document

Many applications scan a document for you. For example, you can use the Paint application that comes with Windows to perform a scan. However, you don't need a special application to perform this task — you can perform it directly in the Devices and Printers window using the following steps:

1. **Right-click the scanning device you want to use in the Devices and Printers window, and choose Start Scan from the context menu.**

   You see the New Scan dialog box. (See Figure 7-8.)

2. **If the Scanner field entry is wrong, click Change.**

   You see the Select Device dialog box, as shown in Figure 7-9. The following steps tell how to configure the scanner entries.

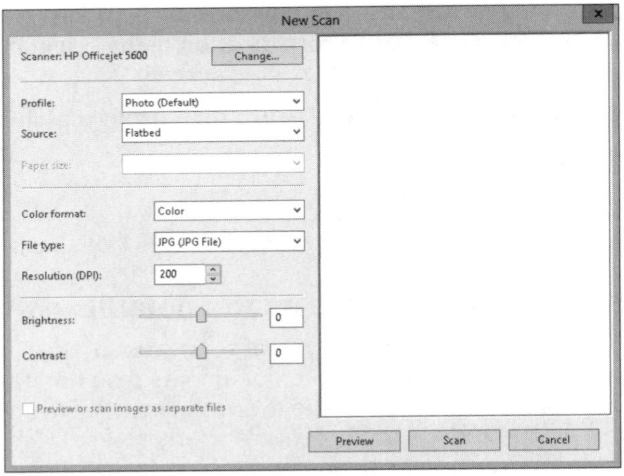

**Figure 7-8**

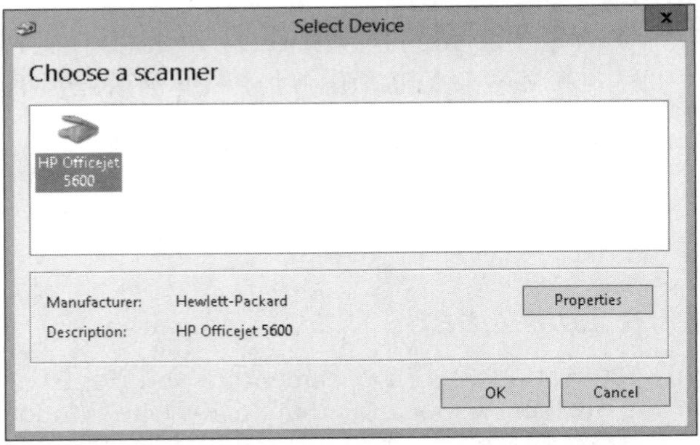

**Figure 7-9**

   *a. Select the scanning device you want to use.*

   You see basic information about the device.

   *b. (Optional) Click Properties, modify any required properties, and then click OK.*

   You see the device's Properties dialog box, where you can change specific information about the device. In addition, this dialog box provides features for testing the scanner.

   *c. Click OK.*

   Windows selects the new device and displays its name in the Scanner field.

3. **Select the profile you want to use from the Profile list.**

The New Scan dialog box automatically changes all scan configuration features to match the profile you select.

4. **Make any required changes to the scanner configuration.**

5. **When working with the flatbed scanner, place a typical image that you want to scan in the scanner, and then click Preview.**

Windows scans the object for you and displays the result in the preview area.

6. **If the output doesn't reflect the original, adjust the Brightness and Contrast controls as needed to obtain a better result.**

You may not be able to match colors precisely, but you can obtain a close approximation of the original, especially when working with text or grayscale images.

7. **Repeat Steps 5 and 6 until the output matches the original closely.**

8. **Click Scan.**

Windows performs the required scan for you. You see the Import Pictures and Videos dialog box, as shown in Figure 7-10.

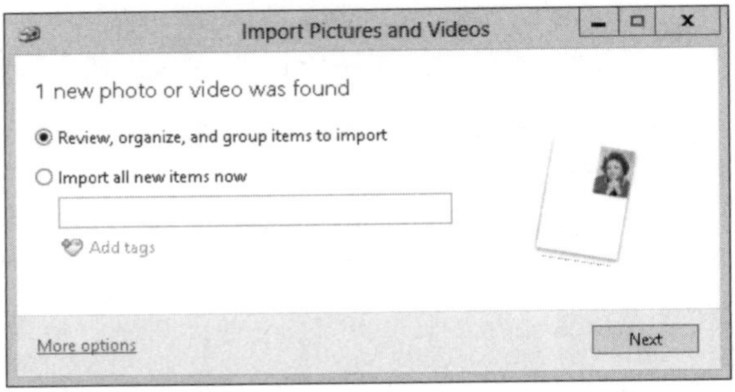

**Figure 7-10**

**9. Click Next.**

Windows asks you to provide a name for each image you want to import, as shown in Figure 7-11. When working with a flatbed scanner, you see only one image. However, when working with a document feeder, you see as many images as the document feeder has scanned for you.

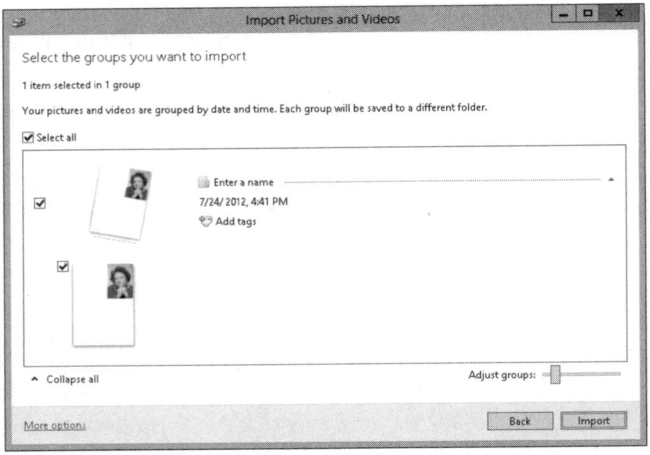

**Figure 7-11**

**10. Type a name for each image and then click Import.**

Windows saves each image in your My Pictures folder with the name you selected for it and in the file format you chose for the profile.

# Working with Pictures

Any device that supports a camera interface that Windows supports can provide access to pictures you take. All you need to do is plug the device into your machine and turn it on. Depending on the device, you may need to tell it to use the Universal Serial Bus (USB) output rather than a direct printer output. Windows automatically recognizes the device, installs support for it as needed, and then provides access to it for you. You see a toast that says *Tap to See What Happens to Memory Card.* Tap the toast and you see the list of options, as shown in Figure 7-12.

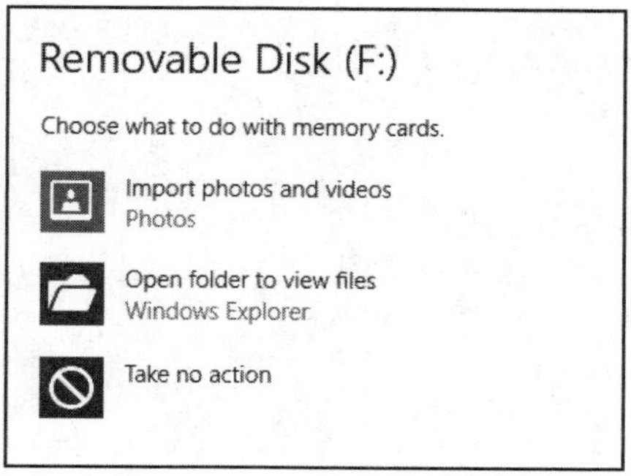

Removable Disk (F:)

Choose what to do with memory cards.

[icon] Import photos and videos
Photos

[icon] Open folder to view files
Windows Explorer

[icon] Take no action

**Figure 7-12**

Of course, you can always choose not to do anything by clicking Take No Action. (As an alternative, you can simply wait for the toast to clear by itself.)

After you select an action the first time, Windows performs the same action every time it detects the camera. Unfortunately, you may want to do something different. In this case, open the Devices and Printers window, right-click the device, and choose Autoplay⊏>Removable Disk from the context menu. You see the menu for choosing an option for interacting with the device again. The following sections assume that you want to do something more with the images on the camera.

## Viewing pictures directly

Most people want to see their pictures immediately — they don't want to play around with the Windows file system. The following steps describe how to obtain access to your pictures immediately and save them to disk for later viewing:

*1.* **Choose the Import Photos and Videos option in the dialog box.**

The Windows 8 app named Photos opens and displays the list of pictures on your device, as shown in Figure 7-13.

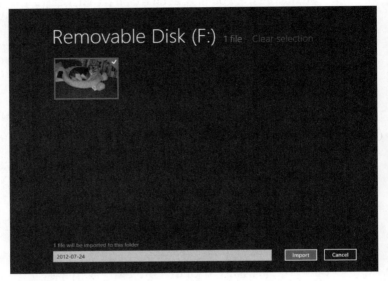

Figure 7-13

*2.* **Click each picture to either add the check mark to it or remove the check mark from it.**

Windows imports each of the pictures you select.

*3.* **In the blank field provided at the bottom of the window, type a name for the folder you want to use to hold the pictures onscreen.**

Windows defaults to providing the current date as the folder name.

*4.* **Click Import.**

Windows creates the required folder for you and then places the pictures in it. When the import process is complete, you see a completion message like the one shown in Figure 7-14.

Figure 7-14

5. **Click Open Album.**

You see the images you've imported.

## Opening the picture folder

Using the Windows file system to view the images on a device offers a level of flexibility that you won't obtain by importing them directly. When working with the file system, you can choose to delete images you don't want or to view images directly on the camera's disk using more than one application. Every feature of the Windows file system is available to you when you use this option (along with the attendant complexity).

In this case, all you need to do is choose Open Folder to View Files when prompted. A copy of Windows Explorer opens and takes you directly to the camera's hard drive. You can see the images as thumbnails and work with them as you would work with any other picture on the hard drive.

# *Accessing the Network*

Many computers today are networked in some way. Even a home system often belongs to a network because each person has a separate system that shares resources with other systems in the house. In fact, some people may have multiple systems in their house, each of which serves a different purpose. No matter how your systems are networked, it's important to know how to interact with the network to gain access to the resources you need.

This part describes some of the more essential network features that you interact with when working with Windows. When you complete this part, you'll have the skills required to define a basic network or connect with an enterprise network.

## In this part . . .

- ✓ Adding a Network Connection
- ✓ Becoming Part of a Domain
- ✓ Becoming Part of a Workgroup
- ✓ Configuring a HomeGroup
- ✓ Configuring the Firewall
- ✓ Connecting to Remote Resources
- ✓ Interacting with Windows Defender

# Adding a Network Connection

Generally, Windows detects and configures your machine to access the network. In fact, it often locates and configures your Internet connection as well. However, sometimes you need to configure a network connection manually. Perhaps you need to set up a network connection before you leave on a business trip, or the network you plan to connect to isn't active at the moment.

You *must* install any required equipment and supporting device drivers before you begin this procedure. Make sure that you know the connection details for the kind of connection you want to create. For example, when working with an Internet connection, you need connection details from your Internet provider. A workplace connection requires connection details from the network administrator at your workplace. The following steps help you create a network connection when Windows doesn't detect it automatically:

1. **Open the Control Panel.**

2. **Click View Network Status and Tasks within the Network and Internet group.**

    You see the Network and Sharing Center window, as shown in Figure 8-1. Notice that the window provides status information fvor any current network connections.

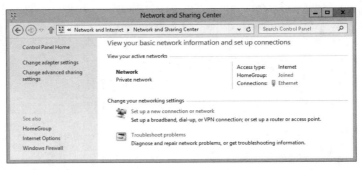

**Figure 8-1**

3. **Click Set Up a New Connection or Network.**

    The Set Up a Connection or Network Wizard starts, as shown in Figure 8-2. The wizard helps you create one of three network connection types: Internet, local, or workplace.

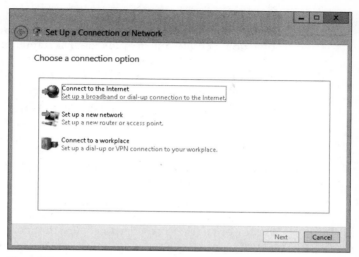

**Figure 8-2**

Each of these setup routines is smart. For example, if you try to set up a new local connection, and Windows doesn't find a router or another access point to support it, the wizard simply waits for the device to connect or, eventually, displays an error message. When you already have an Internet connection, the wizard tells you that this connection exists and ensures that you want to set up another one, as shown in Figure 8-3.

When you see a condition like this, consider the following reasons:

- The equipment you need in order to create the connection isn't installed, turned on, or active.

- Windows is waiting for you to install device drivers to support the device used to access the network connection. (See the "Adding Device Support" section in Part 7 for details.)

- You've selected the wrong connection type.

4. **Choose connection details for the kind of connection you want to create.**

Each connection type requires that you provide connection details that are available from the network provider. For example, a workplace connection requires that you know whether you need to connect using a modem or a virtual private network (VPN). In most cases, you need some connectivity information, such as a telephone number for a modem connection or an Internet address for a VPN. Providing these sorts of details is outside the scope of this book.

5. **After you complete the connection details (usually contained on multiple pages of the wizard), click Create.**

   Windows creates the new connection for you.

6. **When the network is already active, use the new connection to connect to the network.**

   You see the expected resources. If you don't see them but the connection succeeds, contact the network administrator or another provider to ensure that connection security and other configuration details are correct.

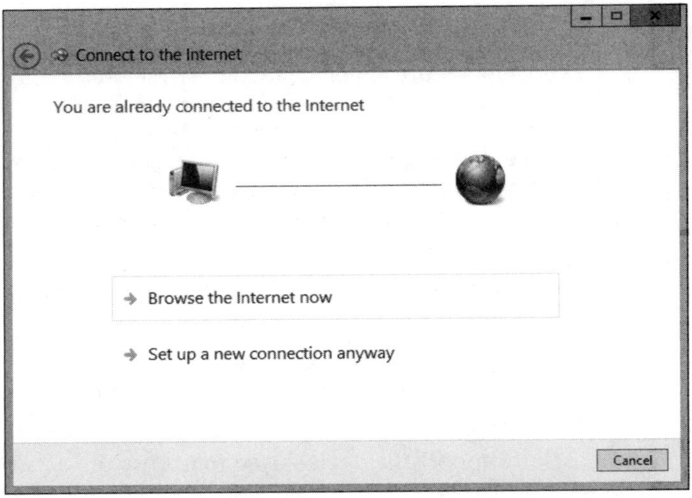

Figure 8-3

# *Becoming Part of a Domain*

Domains are used for large networks in the enterprise environment and they help administrators manage a large number of systems with less work. When Windows detects a local area network (LAN) connection, it connects your system to the network as a workgroup connection. Domain-related features, such as Active Directory, are then unavailable when you initially start using the connection. To access these features, you must join the domain.

Unlike workgroups, domains are normally based around dedicated servers. When a client logs in to a server, the server can provide access to resources that it controls. The use of dedicated servers also means that an administrator normally has better control over security and resource usage. The following steps detail one method of joining a domain:

1. **Open the Control Panel.**

2. **Click the System and Security group.**

   You see the System and Security window.

3. **Click the System group.**

   You see the System window.

4. **Click Advanced System Settings.**

   You see the System Properties dialog box.

5. **Choose the Computer Name tab.**

   You see the computer's name and workgroup, as shown in Figure 8-4.

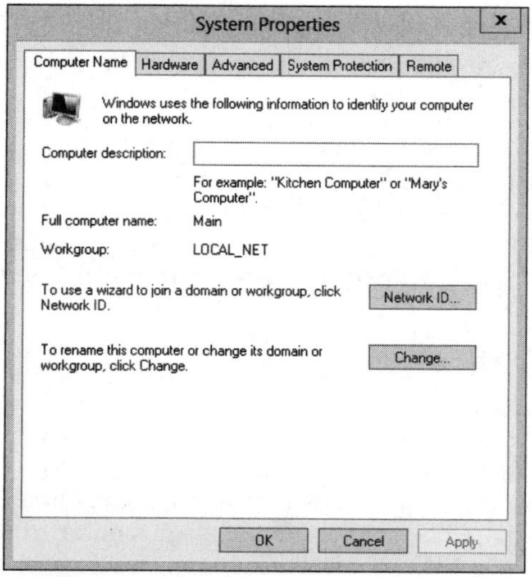

**Figure 8-4**

6. **Click Network ID.**

   The Join a Workgroup or Domain Wizard starts. You can use this wizard to join a workgroup, but using the technique shown in the previous section is much easier. Because a domain requires additional information, using the wizard is a better choice when working with a domain.

7. **Choose the option labeled This Computer Is Part of a Business Network; I Use It to Connect to Other Computers at Work, and click Next.**

   The wizard asks whether your network is part of a domain.

8. **Choose the My Computer Uses a Network with a Domain option and click Next.**

   The next page of the wizard tells you about items of information that you need in order to join a domain. You must have this information on hand before you do anything else. If necessary, ask your network administrator for the information you need.

9. **Click Next.**

   The wizard asks you for your login information, as shown in Figure 8-5. Notice that you must provide a domain name as part of the information. The domain name tells which domain can authenticate your account.

10. **Type the name, password, and domain name needed to log in to the server.**

    It's important to realize that you may use a login name and password to log in to the domain that are different from the ones you use on your personal system. When you find that you have trouble logging in, make sure that you check your login information to ensure that it's correct.

11. **Click Next.**

    Windows attempts to verify your association with the domain. Unlike a workgroup, a server must recognize your name and password in order for you to join a domain. When Windows can verify your domain information, it displays a welcome message similar to the one that's provided when you join a workgroup. However, when Windows can't verify your domain membership, it provides a series of troubleshooting dialog boxes to help you join the domain. Simply follow the troubleshooting dialog boxes until you succeed in joining the domain. Step 12 assumes that you've joined the domain and that you're seeing the welcome message for the domain.

**12. Click OK.**

You see another message box stating that you must reboot the computer for the changes to take effect.

**13. Click OK.**

**14. Click Close in the System Properties dialog box.**

You see a message box asking whether you want to start the system now or later.

**15. Click Restart Now.**

The system restarts. After you log back in to the system, your machine is part of the domain whose name you provided.

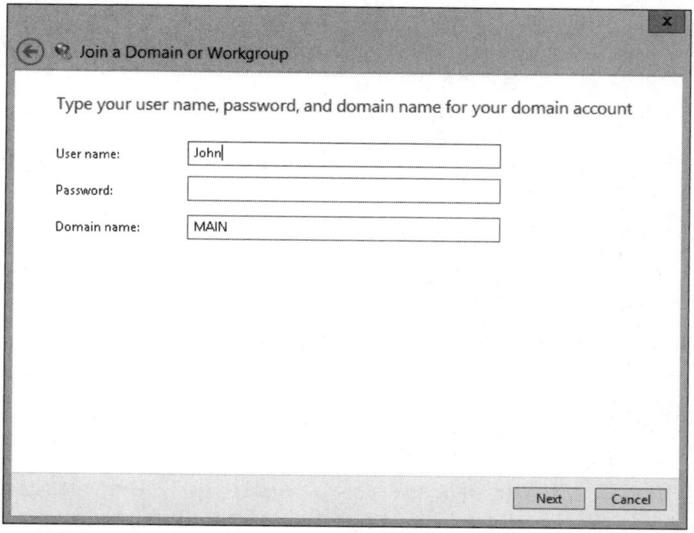

**Figure 8-5**

# Becoming Part of a Workgroup

Home networks and smaller work networks are usually created as workgroups because managing a workgroup is far easier than managing a domain, and it also requires less software. Workgroups provide a cozy group that can share resources, such as printers, equally. In a workgroup, any system can act as both a *server* (a machine that provides resources to other machines) and a *client* (a machine that request resources from a server). When you install Windows, it assumes that you want to join a workgroup named Workgroup, which is seldom the case. So this is one time when you must configure the machines on your network to use the same workgroup. All you need to do to create the workgroup is assign the machine to it, as described in the following steps:

1. **Open the Control Panel.**

2. **Click the System and Security group.**

   You see the System and Security window.

3. **Click the System group.**

   You see the System window.

4. **Click Advanced System Settings.**

   You see the System Properties dialog box.

5. **Choose the Computer Name tab.**

   You see the computer's name and workgroup, as shown earlier in Figure 8-4.

6. **Click Change.**

   You see the Computer Name/Domain Changes dialog box, as shown in Figure 8-6.

7. **Select the Workgroup option. Type the name of your workgroup in the associated field and then click OK.**

   After a few moments, you see a message box welcoming you to the workgroup you typed.

   Windows always welcomes you to the workgroup name you provide, even if you type the workgroup name incorrectly. Make absolutely certain that you type the workgroup name correctly, or else you can end up in your own, personal workgroup rather than as part of the workgroup whose resources you want to share.

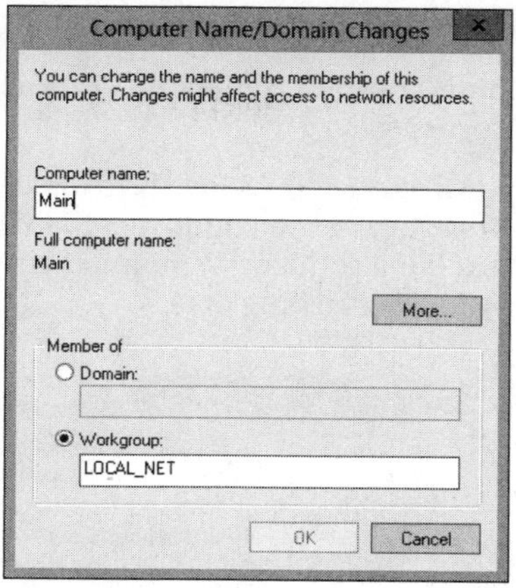

**Figure 8-6**

> *8.* **Click OK.**
>
>   You see another message box stating that you must reboot the computer for the changes to take effect.
>
> *9.* **Click OK.**
>
> *10.* **Click Close in the System Properties dialog box.**
>
>   You see a message box asking whether you want to start the system now or later.
>
> *11.* **Click Restart Now.**
>
>   The system restarts. After you log back in to the system, your machine is part of the workgroup whose name you provided.

# Configuring a HomeGroup

A *HomeGroup* is a location where you can place data items to share with other people. Every member of the HomeGroup has access to the items shared as part of the HomeGroup. The physical location of the data is unimportant because you access it as part of the HomeGroup. Windows tracks the physical location — all you worry about is the data itself. However, before you can share resources with a HomeGroup, you must configure the HomeGroup for use as described in the following steps:

*1.* **Open the Control Panel.**

*2.* **Click Choose HomeGroup and Sharing Options in the Network and Internet group.**

You see the HomeGroup window, as shown in Figure 8-7. Notice that the first step in the window is highlighted and marked with an exclamation icon. You must complete this step before you do anything else.

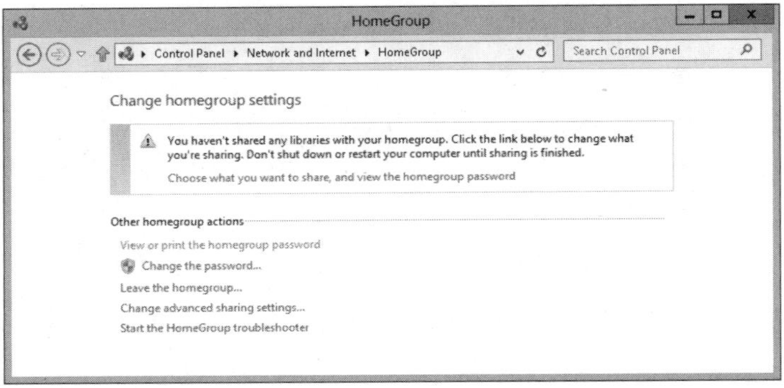

HomeGroup

Control Panel ▸ Network and Internet ▸ HomeGroup            Search Control Panel

Change homegroup settings

⚠ You haven't shared any libraries with your homegroup. Click the link below to change what you're sharing. Don't shut down or restart your computer until sharing is finished.
Choose what you want to share, and view the homegroup password

Other homegroup actions

View or print the homegroup password
Change the password...
Leave the homegroup...
Change advanced sharing settings...
Start the HomeGroup troubleshooter

**Figure 8-7**

*3.* **Click Choose What You Want to Share, and View the HomeGroup Password.**

Windows starts the HomeGroup Wizard. The first page of this wizard asks what you want to share, as shown in Figure 8-8.

*4.* **Select the items you want to share and then click Next.**

Windows generates a password for you that meets the specifications of being hard to guess and displays it onscreen. Unfortunately, the password is also hard to remember, making it necessary for you to write it down.

Creating a complex password that's hard to guess is important because you don't want outsiders accessing the resources you make available to the HomeGroup. However, you also need a password that you can easily remember, such as Luv2S#are!. Click Change the Password in the HomeGroup window after you complete this wizard to give your HomeGroup a complex password that's also easy to remember.

5.  **Click Finish.**

Your HomeGroup is now ready for use.

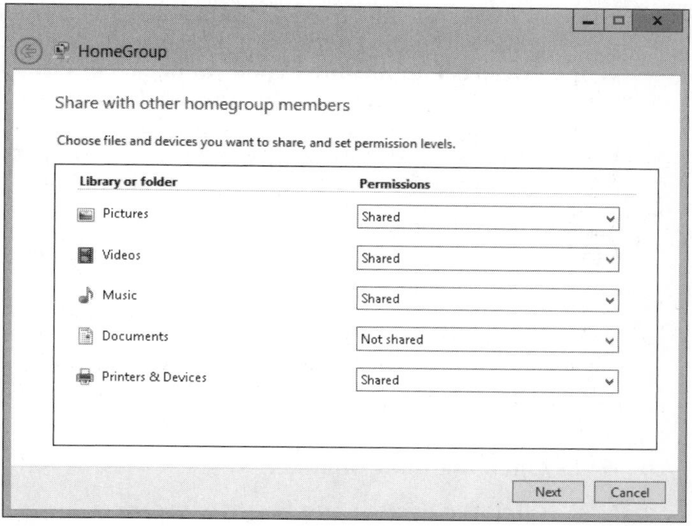

**Figure 8-8**

To view the content of the HomeGroup, open a copy of File Explorer and select the HomeGroup folder in the Navigation (left) pane. The HomeGroup is organized by user, machine, and then content that the user has shared, as shown in Figure 8-9. When you want to find content from a specific user, open that user's folder, drill down into the machine that the user has used to store the data, and then choose the specific content you want.

**Figure 8-9**

# Configuring the Firewall

The Windows Firewall can help prevent certain kinds of outside threats from gaining access to your machine. A firewall doesn't typically stop someone from sending you a virus or causing your browser to go to a virus site. However, a firewall can prevent an external application from gaining access to your system. In addition, in some situations, a firewall can also prevent an application on your system from gaining unauthorized access to outside resources. The firewall is part of an overall protection strategy for your system, but not the only part.

Many organizations rely on a third-party firewall with more features than the Windows Firewall provides. Before you configure your firewall, make sure you understand how the security features of your system are configured. When in doubt, check with the network administrator first to ensure that the Windows Firewall is actually in use on your system. The following steps tell you how to check your firewall and perform a few configuration tasks with it to ensure optimal operation:

1. **Open the Control Panel.**

2. **Click the System and Security group.**

   You see the System and Security window.

3. **Click the Windows Firewall group.**

   You see the Windows Firewall window, as shown in Figure 8-10. This window provides access to all the Windows Firewall configuration features and also shows the firewall status.

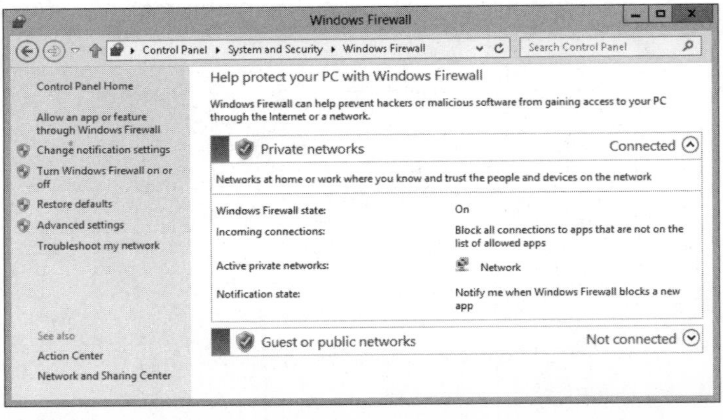

**Figure 8-10**

4. **Verify that the Windows Firewall is On and configured for the kind of network environment you use.**

   You typically need to verify that the firewall is on, that it generates the kinds of notifications you need, and that it allows applications you trust to access outside resources.

## Allowing applications through the firewall

Windows Firewall normally notifies you when it blocks application or feature access to outside resources. In some cases, you may find that an application or a feature that would normally work isn't behaving as expected. When you suspect that the application or feature lacks access to a resource, use these steps to grant it access to the required resource:

1. **Click Allow an App or Feature Through Windows Firewall.**

   You see the Allowed Apps window, as shown in Figure 8-11.

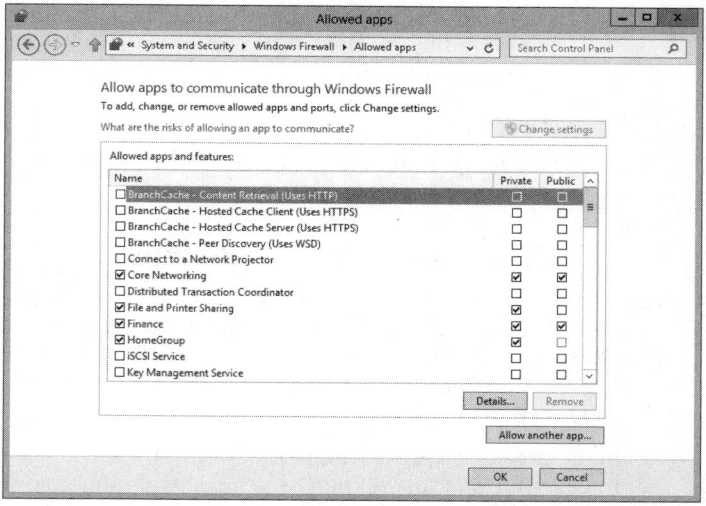

**Figure 8-11**

2. **Place a check mark next to any application or feature entries that you want to allow access to external resources.**

Windows automatically places a check mark in the Public or Private column as needed, based on the kind of network that's connected to your system. A *public network* is one that's connected to a shared network in a public setting, such as a coffeehouse or bookstore. A *private network* is one that's connected to a secured network at home or in a workplace.

3. **(Optional) Place or remove check marks in the Public and Private columns associated with the application or feature entry.**

Changing the check mark from the default setting allows or disallows access in a particular setting. For example, if you want to allow access when connected to a private network, but not when connected to a public network, place a check mark in the Private column and remove it in the Public column.

If you don't know the task that a particular app or feature performs, select the app or feature in the list and click Details. Windows displays a short description of that app or feature to you (when available — the vendor must provide the required information as part of writing the app or feature code).

4. **Click OK.**

Windows modifies the rights of the applications you changed to access external resources.

## Modifying the firewall notifications

The default setting tells Window Firewall to notify you whenever it blocks an app or a feature from accessing external resources. To check the status of this setting, click Change Notification Settings. You see the Customize Settings window, as shown in Figure 8-12.

In most cases, this feature works well. You see a message every time Windows Firewall blocks access, and you have the choice of allowing access. However, you may not be at your desk to respond to the blocked-access message, or the vendor who wrote the app or feature may try to access an external resource in a way that Windows Firewall doesn't detect. Despite these limitations, it's generally a good idea to tell Windows Firewall to notify you.

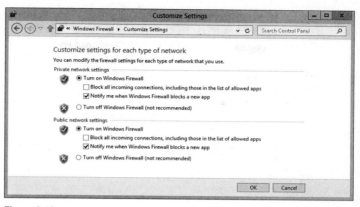

**Figure 8-12**

Public networks can be an exception to the rule. Notice that one setting blocks all access to your system. This option is useful in settings where you don't trust the network connection you're using. In unsafe public settings, the smart choice is to block all access and then tell Windows Firewall not to tell you about any blocked access so that you can continue working without constant interruption.

## Turn the firewall on

Windows defaults to turning on the firewall for you from the outset. If you don't install another firewall, or you have a virus infection, or you turn off the firewall manually, the firewall normally remains on. If you check the firewall and find it turned off, you should turn it back on unless you have a third-party firewall performing the same task. To change the status of this setting, click Turn Windows Firewall On or Off. You see the Customize Settings window, shown earlier in Figure 8-12. Choose the Turn on Windows Firewall option and click OK.

# Connecting to Remote Resources

Part 7 of this book tells how to work with local printers and other devices connected to your system. In some cases, you need access to devices connected to other systems. When the user of that system shares the device, you can access it through the network connection. To see the resources that other machines have to share, open a copy of File Explorer and select the Network folder, or double-click the Network icon on the Desktop to open it. Select the machine that has the resource you want to connect to and you see resource icons such as drives and printers, as shown in Figure 8-13. Each of these icons represents a *share* — a resource that's shared among users of a workgroup or domain.

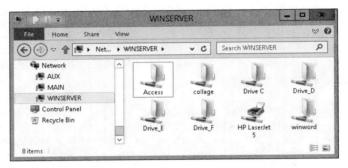

**Figure 8-13**

You need the proper rights to access these resources. If you don't have the proper rights, Windows tells you that it can't access the resource and asks for the name and password of an account that can access the resource. The following sections describe how to access the two most common resources: printers and drives.

## Accessing remote printers

The price of printers has dropped considerably, but you still may not want to buy a printer for every computer in the house. Sharing a printer makes sense because not everyone uses the printer constantly.

When you want to access a remote printer, right-click the resource you want to share and choose Connect from the context menu. You see the Windows Printer Installation dialog box appear. Windows searches for an appropriate device driver for the printer and installs it on your machine.

## Working with remote drives

The most common way to share files in a workgroup or domain is to place the files in a central location, create a share for that location, and then ask everyone to connect to that share. For the share to appear in File Explorer, like your local drives, you must map the drive. *Mapping a drive* is the act of telling Windows to access a remote share and giving it a local drive letter. The following steps tell how to map a drive:

1. **Right-click the drive you want to map in the Network folder of File Explorer and choose Map Network Drive from the context menu.**

   You see the Map Network Drive dialog box, as shown in Figure 8-14.

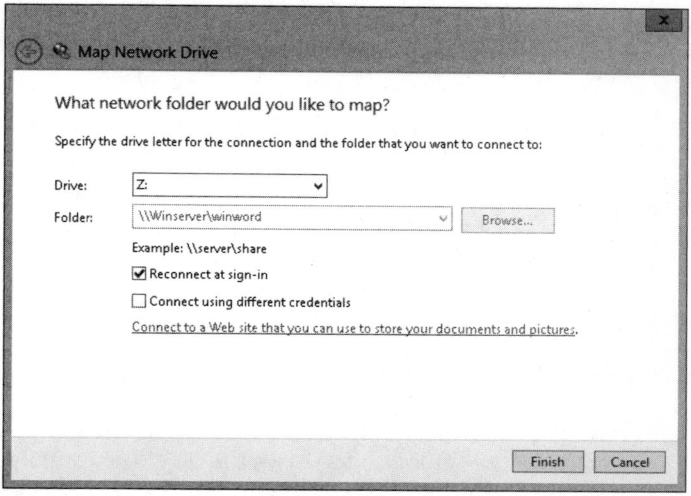

Map Network Drive

What network folder would you like to map?

Specify the drive letter for the connection and the folder that you want to connect to:

Drive:  Z:

Folder:  \\Winserver\winword        Browse...

Example: \\server\share

☑ Reconnect at sign-in

☐ Connect using different credentials

Connect to a Web site that you can use to store your documents and pictures.

Finish    Cancel

**Figure 8-14**

2. **Choose the local drive you want to use to access the remote drive in the Drive list.**

   Your system supports drive letters from A through Z. Letters A and B are used for older, removable media drives. Letter C is used for the first hard drive on your system, and Letter D is used for the first DVD drive when you have no other hard drives. In short, local drives begin with A and move toward Z. Network drives normally begin with the letter Z and move backward through the list.

3. **Check Reconnect at Sign-In when you plan to use the drive repeatedly.**

4. **Check Connect Using Different Credentials when you need to provide a name and password other than your own to access the drive.**

5. **Click Finish.**

   If you selected the Connect Using Different Credentials option, you see the Windows Security dialog box. The following steps tell how to configure this dialog box:

   a. *Type the name and password of the account you plan to use to access the drive.*

   b. *Select Remember My Credentials if you plan to use the same name and password every time you access the drive.*

   c. *Click OK.*

      Windows verifies that that name and password you provided will work to access the drive.

   Windows maps the drive for you. You see it displayed in File Explorer and you can access it as you would access any local drive.

# Interacting with Windows Defender

*Windows Defender* is the free virus-protection application that comes with Windows. It provides protection against many outside threats. In addition, it scans your drive to look for files containing viruses or other threats that you may have installed or inadvertently downloaded. Windows turns on Windows Defender by default when you install Windows in order to provide constant protection. Perform the following steps to see the Windows Defender window:

1. **Press Win.**

   Windows displays the Start screen.

2. **Right-click the Start screen and choose All Apps from the App bar.**

   You see the Apps screen.

3. **Click Windows Defender in the Windows System group.**

   You see the Windows Defender application start, as shown in Figure 8-15.

**Figure 8-15**

The application always opens to the Home tab, which provides you with an overview of the Windows Defender status. You can also start a scan of your hard drive from this tab by selecting a scan option and clicking Scan Now.

Windows Defender automatically updates itself as needed. If you think that the virus protection may be outdated, select the Update tab and click Update. Windows Defender looks online for any updates, and then downloads and installs them as needed.

Whenever Windows Defender detects a threat, it asks you immediately what to do about that threat. After you select an action, Windows Defender quarantines, deletes, or ignores the file. The History tab of the Windows Defender window lets you review the actions you took with specific files. When working with quarantined files, you can highlight a file entry in the list and choose to either remove or restore the file as needed.

The Settings tab, shown in Figure 8-16, provides access to the Windows Defender configuration. If you install third-party virus protection on your system, it's usually best to turn off Windows Defender to keep the two applications from clashing. To do this, clear the check mark from the Turn On Real-Time Protection option in the Real-Time Protection folder.

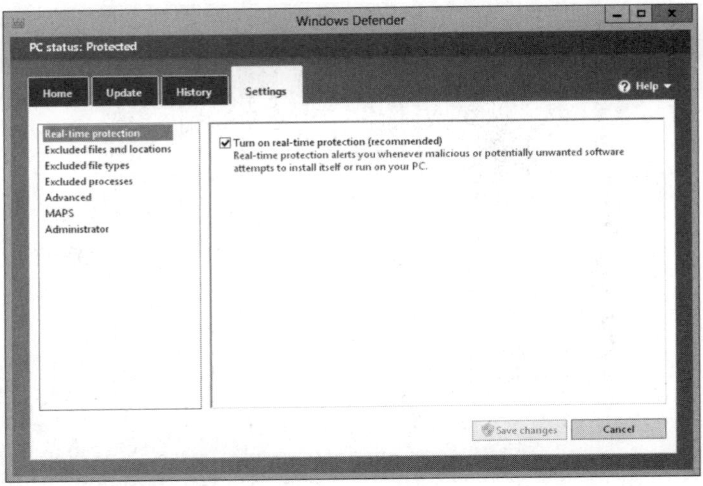

**Figure 8-16**

Some files are perfectly benign, yet Windows Defender tries to flag them as virus-ridden. This is a common problem with virus protection, and most people call it a *false positive.* To prevent false positives, you can configure Windows Defender to exclude files and locations, file types, and even processes from the scan.

The Advanced folder contains some useful settings, such as whether you want to scan within archive folders. Perhaps the most useful setting is telling Windows Defender that you want to create a restore point every time it reacts to a detected item by removing, running, or quarantining it. You can also tell Windows Defender to automatically delete quarantined items after a specific interval, which means that you must actually review the quarantined item list from time to time to avoid losing something you want to keep.

# Performing Administrative Tasks

Every system requires some level of administration. Even if you have a single machine, you need to perform tasks such as updating the applications and installing new features. The task of maintaining the system and keeping it ready for use is called *administration,* and on large networks, the task is performed by the administrator.

This part discusses basic administrative tasks that you may need to perform. For example, you need to know how to open a command prompt for those times when someone asks you to type in a command. Some tasks, such as resetting your network adapter when it fails to clear itself, require that you work at the command prompt. Most people also need to *elevate* (obtain additional rights from) their account privileges at times in order to perform special tasks. The Administrative Tools folder of the Control Panel also contains an amazing array of tools for managing and maintaining your system.

## In this part . . .

- Opening a Command Prompt
- Starting Applications with the Administrator Account
- Using the Administrative Tools Folder Consoles
- Using the Remote Desktop to Access a System

# Opening a Command Prompt

A *command prompt* is a special kind of window where you can type keywords that perform tasks without using the Windows graphical interface. At one time, all computer interaction occurred at the command prompt, but today you need to use the command prompt only for special tasks. The following sections tell how to start the command prompt and use it to perform common tasks. You also see how to ask the command prompt for help when you need it.

## Adding a command prompt entry to the Start menu

The command prompt is one application that doesn't appear on the Start menu by default. Use the following steps to create a command prompt:

1. **Press Win.**

   Windows displays the Start screen.

2. **Right click the Start screen and choose All Apps from the App bar.**

   You see the Apps screen.

3. **Click Command Prompt in the Windows System group.**

   Windows creates a command prompt for you.

If you need to perform administrative tasks regularly or you simply find that the command prompt makes it easier to perform certain tasks, you can add it to the Start screen by using the technique discussed in the "Pinning or unpinning an app" section of Part 1.

## Opening a new window

When you start a new copy of the command prompt, you see a window like the one shown in Figure 9-1. (The window is shown with a white background and black letters to make it easier to see in the book — normally, the window has a black background with gray letters.) Unlike a graphical interface, the text interface of the command prompt offers little information.

Windows command prompt version number

System Menu          Copyright notice

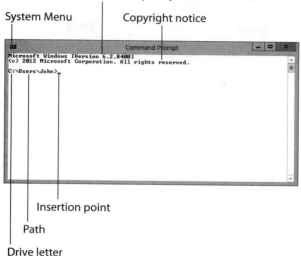

Insertion point

Path

Drive letter

**Figure 9-1**

The first two lines contain the command prompt version number and the Microsoft copyright notice. The command prompt version number is important because Microsoft adds and removes commands in every version of Windows. Knowing the version number can help you determine whether a command is still useful.

Below these two lines is the command prompt, which consists of the drive letter, the current path, and the insertion point where you type commands. Every drive (floppy drive, removable drive, hard drive, DVD, and flash drive, for example) on your system is assigned a letter. To work with that drive, you must know its letter. The *path* is a listing of the hierarchy of folders used to access the current location. You use a path all the time in File Explorer, though you may not think about it much because you're used to seeing the information visually. Figure 9-2 shows this same path in File Explorer.

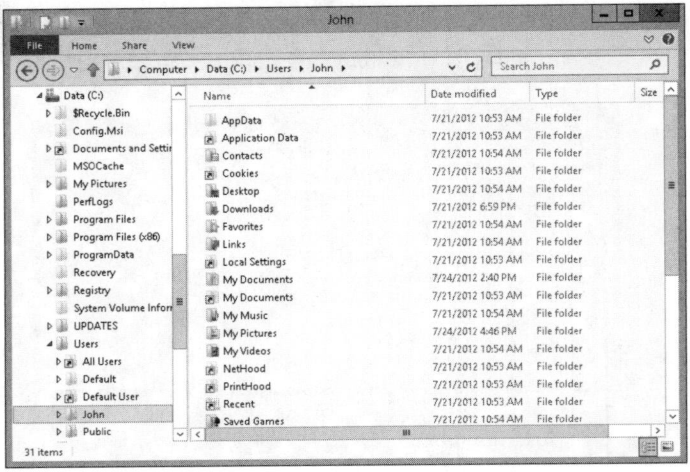

**Figure 9-2**

Notice that the Address field displays the same information as the prompt shown in Figure 9-1, but the information is presented in a different way. Both presentations mean the same thing. The command prompt is currently working with the `John` folder, found in the `Users` folder, on drive C. The *insertion point* indicates where you type text, just as you would in a word processor.

## Opening the Properties dialog box

The command prompt has a number of properties associated with it. For example, you can change the colors used for the background and the text. You can also adjust the size of the window and the size of the text used to display information. Many people never use the System menu because it simply isn't necessary with most applications. When working with the command prompt, it becomes necessary to work with the System menu in certain situations, such as accessing the Command Prompt properties. Click the System menu and you see a list of options like the ones shown in Figure 9-3.

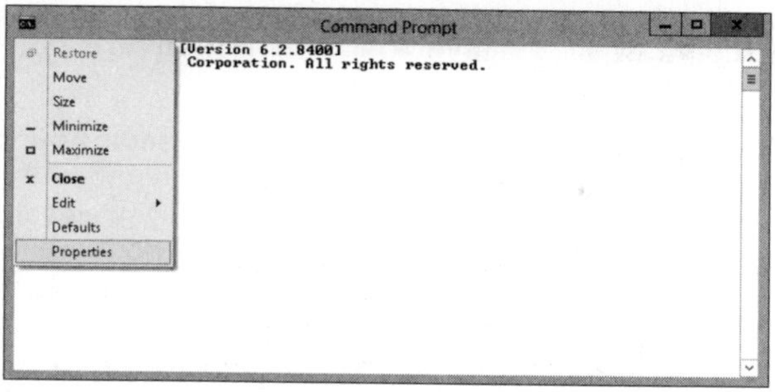

**Figure 9-3**

Notice the Defaults and Properties options on this menu. Click either of these options and you see a Properties dialog box like the one shown in Figure 9-4. However, when you choose Defaults, you change the settings for all Command Prompt windows. On the other hand, when you choose Properties, you change the settings only for Command Prompt windows that have the current title (Command Prompt, in this case). The changes you make don't affect a Command Prompt window with a different title. The difference is noted in the dialog box title — it's Console Window Properties when you select Defaults, and it's Command Prompt Properties when you select Properties.

**Figure 9-4**

The properties appear on four tabs to make them easier to use. Each of these tabs lets you perform basic configuration tasks, as described in the following list:

- ✔ **Options:** Contains controls that determine how the window works. For example, by changing the number of buffers that that command prompt provides, you can adjust the amount of historical information (previous commands) that the application tracks for you. You can also control the appearance of the cursor and whether you can use quick editing commands. *Quick editing* allows you to use the mouse to copy and paste text into the Command Prompt window rather than rely on the Edit submenu (described in the section "Pasting, selecting, copying, and otherwise manipulating text," later in this part).

- ✔ **Font:** Determines the font family and font size used for text in the Command Prompt window. The default settings work for most people, but you may want to use a larger font if you have a hard time seeing the text, or use a smaller size font when you want to see more commands at a time.

- ✔ **Layout:** Modifies the size of the window, the amount of buffer used to hold parts of the window you can't see (but can scroll to), and the position of the window onscreen when you first open it. The default window size of 80 characters by 25 lines works for most people, but when you work with certain commands, such as Windows Management Instrumentation Command (WMIC), a larger buffer makes it easier to see the information and interact with it.

- ✔ **Colors:** Specifies the colors used for the background and foreground. You can also control the colors of any pop-ups that the command prompt uses. (This feature is rarely used.)

## Pasting, selecting, copying, and otherwise manipulating text

The System menu has another option you need to know about because it can save you considerable time. It's possible to copy something from another window, such as a command you see on a site in your browser, and paste it into the Command Prompt window. It's also possible to mark (select) text in the command prompt and paste it elsewhere. The secret is on the Edit submenu of the System menu:

- ✔ **Mark:** Changes the cursor so that it highlights the text you select using the mouse cursor.

- ✔ **Copy:** Copies to the Clipboard anything you have highlighted in the Command Prompt window. As an alternative, you can press Enter to copy highlighted text to the Clipboard.

- ✔ **Paste:** Pastes any text found on the Clipboard to the Command Prompt window.

- ✔ **Select All:** Highlights all the text you can see in the Command Prompt window.

- ✔ **Scroll:** Makes it possible to scroll to text you can't see when highlighting text.

- ✔ **Find:** Helps you find any text in the Command Prompt window by highlighting it for you.

## Seeking help

Using the command prompt requires knowledge of commands and the command line switches used to modify their behavior. Of course, there are hundreds of commands, and no one can possibly remember them all. Consequently, you need to know how to ask for help with remembering how to use specific commands. Most commands make it possible to obtain help by specifying the / ? command line switch. For example, if you want to see the content of the current folder (or *directory,* in command prompt terms), you use the Dir (for directory) command. However, you need to know more than that command to make your search effective, so you use the / ? command line switch to display Help information, as shown in Figure 9-5.

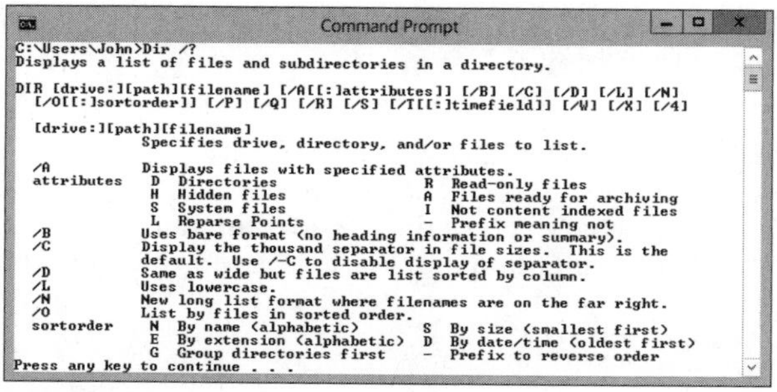

**Figure 9-5**

The Help screen tells you how to use all options that a command provides. Optional items, such as the /A command line switch, appear in square brackets ([ ]). When you see a word, such as *attributes,* you need to replace it with a value. For example, the /AD command line switch displays only the directories (folders) in a particular place. Notice that the word *attributes* appears within a second set of square brackets. You must start the command line switch with /A and then add the attributes, such as D for directory. A third set of square brackets contains an option symbol — the colon (:), in this case. You may, optionally, type /A:D as the command line switch.

Most Help screens begin with the command syntax, which is this part of the Help screen:

```
DIR [drive:][path][filename] [/A[[:]attributes]] [/B]
    [/C] [/D] [/L] [/N] [/O[[:]sortorder]] [/P] [/Q] [/R]
    [/S] [/T[[:]timefield]] [/W] [/X] [/4]
```

The *syntax* shows the overall order of the command and describes how it should appear onscreen. After the syntax, you see the description of each syntax element, such as the use of the attributes.

The Dir command provides only one level of Help because it isn't a complicated command. Some commands are extremely complex and require multiple Help levels. For example, the Net command tells you about your network and helps you manage it. When you type the first level of this command's Help syntax, Net /?, you see the output shown in Figure 9-6, which isn't particularly helpful.

**Figure 9-6**

To find out what each of these subcommands means, you must extend the Help command. For example, when you use the Net Use /? command, you see the extended Help information shown in Figure 9-7.

```
C:\Users\John>Net Use /?
The syntax of this command is:

NET USE
[devicename : *] [\\computername\sharename[\volume] [password : *]]
        [/USER:[domainname\]username]
        [/USER:[dotted domain name\]username]
        [/USER:[username@dotted domain name]
        [/SMARTCARD]
        [/SAVECRED]
        [[/DELETE] : [/PERSISTENT:{YES : NO}]]

NET USE {devicename : *} [password : *] /HOME

NET USE [/PERSISTENT:{YES : NO}]


C:\Users\John>_
```

Figure 9-7

## Using commands

The command line provides access to extremely powerful commands that help you manage your system with a speed that graphical interfaces can't begin to match. Experienced network administrators rely heavily on the command line to accomplish work quickly and with less fuss than using a graphical interface. The price you pay for this speed is that you must know how to use the command, how to seek help when needed, and when not to experiment. The command line is an unforgiving environment that doesn't ask you whether you're certain that you want to do something — it assumes that you are.

The Dir command is one of the easiest commands to experiment with because you can't type anything that will cause damage to your system. For example, if you want to find only the system files and you want them sorted by size, type **Dir / AS /OS** and press Enter. You see output similar to that shown in Figure 9-8. (Your output will be different from mine.)

Notice how quickly you can find the desired information. As you gain experience with the command line, you find that you can locate information even faster than you could start a graphical application to perform the task. The command output shows the date and time that the file or directory was created, the size of the file or the kind of directory entry, and the file or directory name. Try some of the other command line switches to see how this works for you.

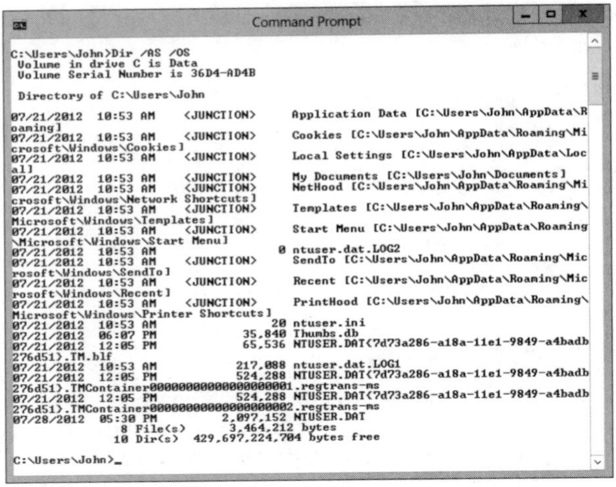

**Figure 9-8**

# *Starting Applications with the Administrator Account*

Microsoft has followed the principle of *least rights* since the introduction of Windows Vista. This term means that your administrator account doesn't have full administrator privileges. To keep your system safe, your account doesn't have full access to every task it can perform unless you *elevate* your privileges. You may have already noticed that when you run certain applications, Windows asks whether you want the application to be able to make changes to your computer through the User Account Control dialog box. When you click Yes, Windows elevates your privileges for that particular application so that the application has access to the full set of rights provided by your administrator account. If you don't have an administrator account, you provide credentials for an administrator account that Windows uses for that application.

Some applications don't ask for privilege elevation. In some cases, you can use the application in a limited way without requesting such elevation so that the application doesn't ask. In other cases, the application is older and doesn't know to ask about elevating your privileges. When this second situation occurs, the application may not even run until you elevate its privileges. The following sections discuss how to run an application with elevated privileges in both the Start screen and Desktop interface.

## Working from the Start screen

As a general rule, Windows 8 apps don't require (or even allow) you to run them with elevated privileges. However, you can start Desktop interface applications from the Start screen with elevated privileges as needed. For example, you may find that certain tools in the Administrative Tools folder (discussed in the section "Using the Administrative Tools Folder Consoles," later in this part), require privilege elevation before you can use them completely. The following steps tell how to elevate your privileges using the Start screen:

*1.* **Right-click the application icon.**

   Windows checks the application icon, and you see the App bar appear.

*2.* **Click Run As Administrator.**

   Windows starts the application with administrator privileges.

## Working with the Taskbar

Every application you can access from the Taskbar provides the means for privilege elevation. In fact, the "Modifying the configuration manually" section of Part 3 describes how to configure an application to always use administrator privileges for the sake of compatibility. However, some applications work fine without privilege elevation, and you only use them sometimes with it in place. For example, the command prompt falls into this category. You see how to use the `Dir` command in the "Using commands" section, earlier in this part, without privilege elevation. For those times when you need to elevate application privileges to perform specific tasks, you can temporarily elevate privileges from the Taskbar by right-clicking the application icon and choosing Run As Administrator from the context menu.

Some applications detect the increase in privileges and provide you with a visual indicator of increased rights. For example, the command prompt changes its behavior, as shown in Figure 9-9. Notice that the title bar now includes the word *Administrator*. The initial folder also changes to `C:\Windows\system32`.

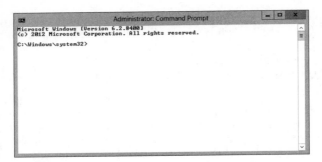

**Figure 9-9**

# Using the Administrative Tools Folder Consoles

The Administrative Tools folder of the Control Panel contains a number of consoles, as shown in Figure 9-10. A *console* is a special kind of configuration file and not truly an application. The underlying application, the Microsoft Management Console (MMC), provides a host environment for *snap-ins*, which are bits of code that provide specific functionality. When you open a console, what you're doing is telling MMC to configure itself with a certain group of snap-ins.

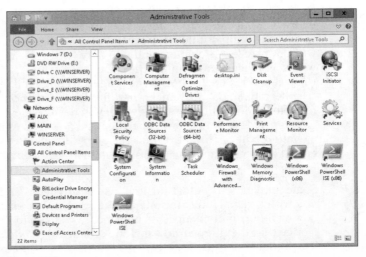

**Figure 9-10**

As its name suggests, the Administrative Tools folder contains tools normally used by the administrator to manage the system. For example, the Computer Management console lets you

- Schedule tasks

- View system events, such as application errors

- Interact with shared resources

- Manage user and group accounts

- Monitor system and application performance

- Access the Device Manager

- Manage the disk drives connected to the system

- Start, stop, and configure system services

- Interact with special applications, such as Windows Management Instrumentation (WMI)

All this functionality comes from a variety of snap-ins. For example, you find the Event Viewer and Services snap-ins used in the Component Services console as well. If you really want to do it, you can create your own custom console that contains the tools you use most often as an administrator. However, a complex topic like this is best left to a book dedicated to Windows management tasks.

# Using the Remote Desktop to Access a System

Administrators normally work with a lot of different machines, not just with the local system. Walking to each of those machines can become time-consuming and prevent the administrator from managing a network efficiently. Fortunately, you have access to a method for interacting with a remote machine as though it were the local machine: The Remote Desktop feature lets you take over the remote system, perform any required tasks, and then end the session to return control to the local user. During the time you work with Remote Desktop, you also have access to local machine features.

Don't confuse Remote Assistance with Remote Desktop. The *Remote Assistance* feature lets you render aid to another user when the user's system is configured to provide this type of access. Using this feature requires that you install a special application on your system so that both you and the user can interact with the remote system. *Remote Desktop,* the ability to use another system from your local machine, lets you take over the remote system and use it as though you were logged on to it locally — only you can interact with the machine. This part discusses Remote Desktop as an aid to administration and not Remote Assistance (as a support aid). You can find detailed information about Remote Assistance at `http://technet.` `microsoft.com/library/bb457004.aspx` and `www.` `tomsitpro.com/articles/remote_desktop_connection-` `windows_8,2-194-2.html`.

## Configuring the remote settings

Windows 8 configures the system by default to allow Remote Assistance access and to disallow Remote Desktop access. To use Remote Desktop, you must configure the system as described in the following steps:

*1.* **Open the Control Panel.**

*2.* **Click System and Security.**

   You see the System and Security window.

*3.* **Click System.**

   You see the System window.

*4.* **Click Remote Settings on the left side of the System window.**

   Windows opens the Remote tab of the System Properties dialog box, as shown in Figure 9-11.

*5.* **Choose the Allow Remote Connections to this Computer option.**

   If you plan to access this system using a version of Windows older than Windows Vista, you must clear the Network Level Authentication (NLA) option that appears below the check box. Only newer versions of Windows support NLA.

Simply selecting this option provides access to anyone with an administrator account. When you want to provide access to users with lesser privileges, you must perform these additional steps:

a. *Click Select Users.*

You see the Remote Desktop Users dialog box, as shown in Figure 9-12.

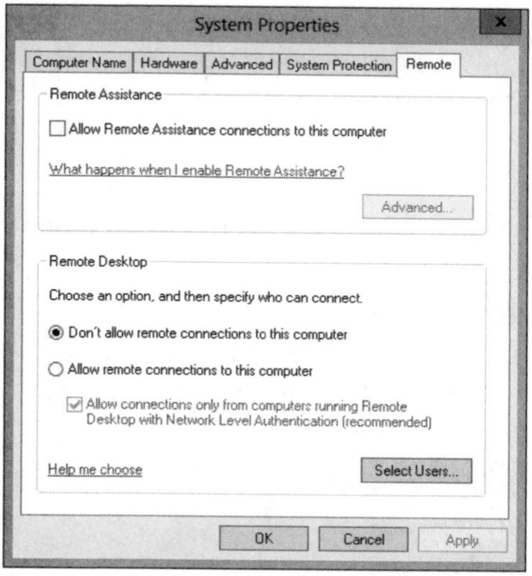

**System Properties** ✕

| Computer Name | Hardware | Advanced | System Protection | Remote |

Remote Assistance

☐ Allow Remote Assistance connections to this computer

What happens when I enable Remote Assistance?

Advanced...

Remote Desktop

Choose an option, and then specify who can connect.

◉ Don't allow remote connections to this computer

○ Allow remote connections to this computer

☑ Allow connections only from computers running Remote Desktop with Network Level Authentication (recommended)

Help me choose                     Select Users...

OK     Cancel     Apply

**Figure 9-11**

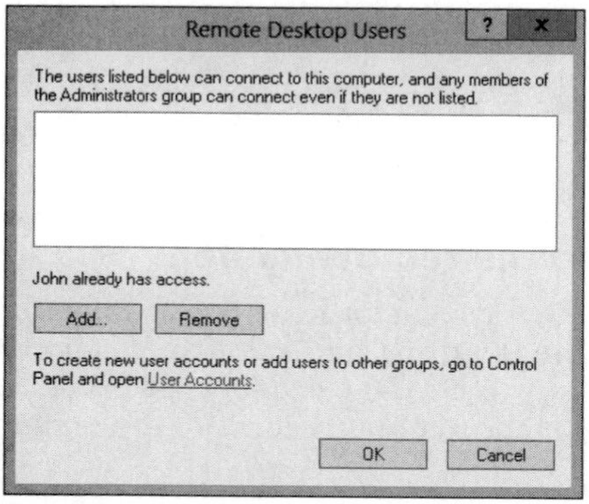

**Remote Desktop Users** ? ✕

The users listed below can connect to this computer, and any members of the Administrators group can connect even if they are not listed.

John already has access.

Add...     Remove

To create new user accounts or add users to other groups, go to Control Panel and open User Accounts.

OK     Cancel

**Figure 9-12**

b. *Click Add.*

You see the Select Users dialog box, as shown in Figure 9-13.

c. *Type the name of the user you want to add and then click Check Names.*

Windows validates the names you've provided.

d. *Click OK.*

You see the names added to the list in the Remote Desktop Users dialog box. If you later decide that you don't want the user to have access to the system, simply highlight the user's name and click Remove.

e. *Click OK.*

Windows provides access to the additional users you selected.

**6. Click OK.**

Windows allows remote desktop access to the system with the configuration information you provided.

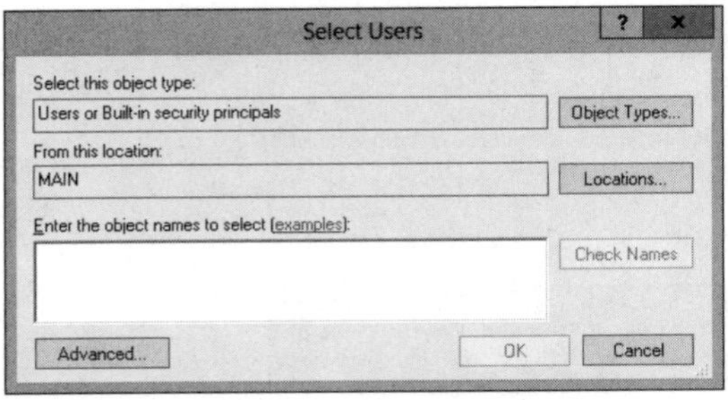

**Figure 9-13**

## Connecting to the remote system

After you configure a system for Remote Desktop access, you can use the Remote Desktop Connection application to access it — assuming that you have the proper rights on that machine. Use the following steps to obtain access to the remote system:

*1.* **Press Win.**

Windows displays the Start screen.

2. **Right-click the Start screen and choose All Apps from the App bar.**

   You see the Apps screen.

3. **Click Remote Desktop Connection in the Windows System group.**

   You see the application start.

4. **Click Show Options.**

   You see the extended set of connection options, as shown in Figure 9-14. It's helpful to configure Remote Desktop Connection before you start a session, to ensure that you get the best performance. You want to provide, at minimum, the computer name, your username, and the level of access you want to local resources (as shown on the Local Resources tab). After you type the account name you want to use, be sure to check the Allow Me to Save Credentials option to save time later when reconnecting to the host system. Also consider modifying the settings on the Display tab to reflect your needs.

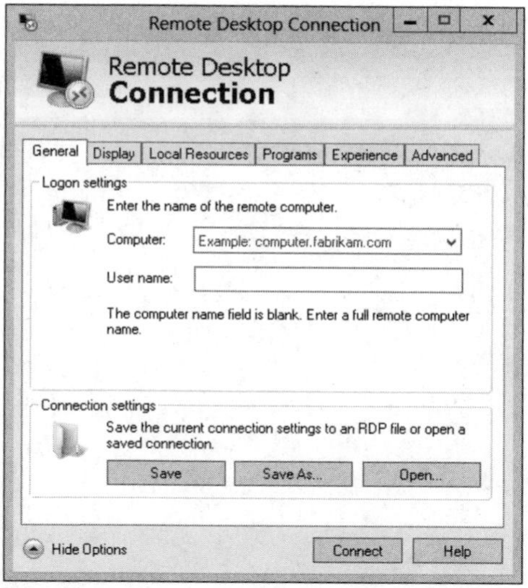

**Figure 9-14**

5. **Configure the connection as required, and then click Save or Save As.**

When you click Save, Windows saves the settings to the default configuration file. When you click Save As, you can save the settings to another Remote Desktop Protocol (.RDP) file. You can later restore these settings by clicking Open and choosing the file you used to save the settings.

6. **Click Connect.**

    Remote Desktop Connection asks you to provide the password needed to access the remote system. You can also use an alternative account when necessary.

7. **Click OK.**

    Remote Desktop Connection connects to the remote system. Figure 9-15 shows a typical example of access to a Windows 2008 system named WinServer. In this case, Remote Desktop connection relied on a windowed interface rather than on a full-screen interface. You can perform any task on this system, including shutting it down. Once you're finished working, log off from the system using the method required by that version of Windows — the Remote Desktop Connection window automatically closes after you're logged out.

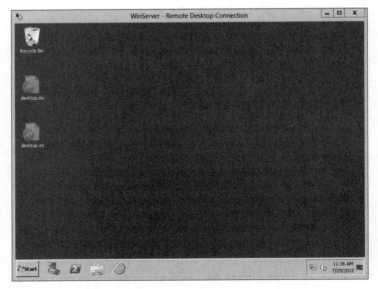

**Figure 9-15**

# Glossary: Tech Talk

**applet:** A special application that appears in the Control Panel and is used to manage Windows. Most applets provide a combination of status information and configuration features.

**cathode ray tube (CRT):** An older technology display that's used to see data managed by the operating system. The CRT relies on an electron beam to excite phosphors on the front of the display to present information. CRT displays are large, bulky, and heavy. They also contain lead and other elements that make disposal difficult. However, many graphic arts and photographic applications still rely on CRT displays because they also provide superior color rendering. *See also* liquid crystal display (LCD).

**charm:** An icon on the Charms bar that provides access to Windows functionality. The individual charms are Search (locates data and applications), Share (lets you share data with others), Start (switches between the Start screen and Desktop interface), Devices (lets you configure devices attached to your system, such as a second monitor), and Settings (provides access to Windows settings).

**client:** A computer element that consumes resources. For example, a client application may request access to a file resource in order to manage the data the file contains. *See also* server.

**console:** An application that provides access to a text-based interface where a user can type commands and receive responses from the applications after they perform the requested task. Console applications typically perform low-level tasks, such as configuring the system or requesting the status of a device. The console provides a fast but unforgiving method of performing tasks efficiently and quickly. *See also* graphical interface and text interface.

**Desktop:** The original interface used by Windows XP and above to provide access to Windows system features, applications, and data. The Desktop interface relies on a desktop model to make the world of computer data seem more like a real desktop in an office.

**device driver:** Specialized low-level code used to aid in communication between a device and the operating system. Each device is unique and requires specialized instructions to perform tasks. The device driver accepts that operating system's standardized instructions and translates them into instructions that the device can understand.

**digital subscriber line (DSL):** One of many methods of providing an Internet connection to computer systems. DSL relies on digital communication over common telephone lines to achieve its purpose. DSL can provide communication upward of 4 megabytes per second (Mb/s); although a speed of 1 Mb/s or 2 Mb/s is more common. To provide this service, the computer must connect to a special DSL modem, and the telephone company must add specialized equipment to the requestor's telephone line. Examples of other sorts of Internet connections are cable and satellite.

**dots per inch (dpi):** A measurement of how many pixels a device can display per inch. The higher the dpi, the less likely the viewer can tell that the output consists of pixels rather than continuous writing. Display adapters normally provide 96 dpi, which is why you can see the individual pixels. Printers commonly provide 300 dpi, 600 dpi, or 1200 dpi, making the output appear printed.

**elevated privileges:** A technique for obtaining rights that are normally denied to the user in order to maintain system security. Windows Vista and later versions use the principle of least privilege (providing the user with the least number of privileges required to perform any given task) to secure the system. However, this approach leaves the user without the rights needed to perform certain tasks, such as an application installation, so elevated privileges become necessary.

**file attribute:** A special addition made to the file information maintained by Windows that describes file characteristics, such as whether the file is a hidden file or a system file. File attributes help the operating system manage the file better and also help the administrator know how to interact with the file.

**firewall:** An application that monitors all requests for network access in the background and blocks any access not specifically granted by the machine's access policy. Using a firewall prevents applications from communicating over the network, especially the Internet, without permission and can help prevent certain types of virus intrusion on your system.

**gadget:** A special application that resides on the Desktop and performs a simple task, such as displaying the time or the weather. A gadget provides continuous information updates in most cases. For example, a gadget designed to monitor the stock market might constantly apprise you of changes in the stocks you monitor.

**gamma:** The relationship between the brightness of a pixel and its numerical value. Pixels are composed of red, blue, and green values between 0 and 255. A pixel with a red value of 127 should appear half as bright as a pixel with a value of 255. However, most displays don't provide this relationship without a gamma correction that adjusts the relationship in brightness to match the pixel's numerical value. *See also* gamma correction.

**gamma correction:** A software- or hardware-based method of modifying the relationship between pixel brightness onscreen and its numerical value. When a user sees a pixel with a value of 127, it should be half as bright as one with a value of 255. This change helps the display adapter output voltages that allow the user to see display elements at the correct brightness level. *See also* gamma.

**graphical interface:** An application output presentation that relies on pictures, icons, and other drawn elements to describe data that the application manages. A graphical interface is interactive, and most users find it easier to work with than a text interface. However, to obtain the usage benefits of a graphical interface, the user normally gives up some efficiency and speed in performing tasks. *See also* text interface.

**Jump List:** An application feature that tracks the documents most recently opened by a user for that particular application. Right-clicking the application's icon presents a list of these documents in a context menu, and clicking the document entry opens the document in that application. A Jump List also provides the means for pinning commonly used documents to the top of the list so that they don't scroll off the bottom of the list when opening a number of documents during any given session.

**liquid crystal display (LCD):** A newer technology display that relies on light shining through crystalline chips to create an image. The crystals permit more or less light to pass through them in order to create the image. LCDs are flat, relatively light, and easier to dispose of than the CRT displays they replace. *See also* cathode ray tube (CRT).

**Live Tiles:** A special type of Windows 8 app tile that provides constant data updates to the tile graphic (in a miniature form). For example, when viewing the News app, you can see news flashes the moment they become available. Likewise, the Weather app shows changes to the weather instantly. *See also* tile.

**local area network (LAN):** A means of connecting computer systems for the purpose of sharing data, applications, and devices within a distance-constrained environment (normally, the same building). Contrast a LAN to the Internet, where a user has access to every server in the world. Businesses use a wealth of network types, including the wide area network (WAN) and the metropolitan area network (MAN).

**Microsoft Management Console (MMC):** An application designed for administrator use that provides no special functionality on its own. Rather, MMC provides a host environment for MMC snap-ins used to create unique management environments that serve specific administrator needs. For example, a snap-in can provide access to the system event log or let the administrator modify user account information. *See also* MMC snap-in.

**MMC snap-in:** A specialized mini-application that relies on the Microsoft Management Console (MMC) application as a host. Each MMC snap-in provides specific functionality for monitoring, configuring, or otherwise managing Windows, devices, applications, or resources. An administrator can combine snap-ins within an MMC console to create a specialized management environment or rely on preconfigured consoles that appear within the `Administrative Tools` folder of the Control Panel. *See also* Microsoft Management Console (MMC).

**Network Level Authentication (NLA):** A protocol used with the Remote Desktop to guarantee that the client and server both identify themselves to ensure that communication takes place between known entities. This security protocol ensures that the two parties are who they say they are. The technique used to perform this task also reduces the potential for a denial-of-service (DoS) attack. Originally, the Remote Desktop relied on server services to establish the identity of the two parties, and a remote client could continuously make connection requests and tie up server resources. Because NLA relies on client services to perform this task, the client's

identity is established before the server becomes involved. *See also* Remote Desktop.

**power usage plan:** A strategy for using power efficiently on a computer system in which all aspects of computer power usage are considered. For example, the plan designates when to turn off the hard drives in order to conserve power. Windows uses the power usage plan to manage system electrical usage and control costs.

**profile:** A collection of configuration settings that determines how the system interacts with a particular resource. Applications and users are the most common targets of profiles for management purposes. Using a profile makes it possible to configure the environment once and then use that custom environment every time the system interacts with the resource. For example, a security profile determines what rights the user has to access a particular resource, such as a file.

**Really Simple Syndication (RSS):** A protocol that establishes a method for communicating content to a client in a push format (where the client doesn't specifically request the information). RSS relies on an eXtensible Markup Language (XML) file to convey specific information about audio, video, graphical, or textual data in a standard format. For example, you can use RSS to receive news feeds or weather reports. An RSS document is commonly called a feed or channel.

**Remote Desktop:** A specialized technology for establishing remote control from one system to another. The client system uses the Remote Desktop Connection application to request a connection with a server system through Remote Desktop Services. When the connection is made, the client system has complete control over the server. A user at the client system can use the server system as though the server system is connected locally. *See also* Network Level Authentication (NLA).

**restore point:** The technology used to safeguard Windows application, setup, and data elements during a system update. If the update fails, restoring the restore point removes the update and returns the system to the state it was in before the update occurred. A restore point assumes that the local hard drive is intact and functional, so it doesn't act as an alternative to creating backups.

**Scalable Vector Graphics (SVG):** A technique for describing two-dimensional graphics information using an XML file. The technique relies on vector graphics (a mathematical description of the image) rather than on raster graphics (actual pixels). Because SVG relies on vectors, the application displaying the graphic can resize it without making the image fuzzy or hard to see. The use of an XML file makes the graphics description fully searchable, and it's possible to compress the file for quicker transmission.

**server:** A computer element that provides resources in response to a client request. For example, a client can request a file that a server has stored on its hard drive. The server would send the data contained in the file to the client for modification and then store those changes to the local file at the client's request. *See also* client.

**Start screen:** A new graphical interface associated with Windows 8 that emphasizes ease of access and simplicity over other considerations.

**text interface:** An application environment that relies entirely on characters rather than on icons, images, or other graphical elements. In most cases, a user types a command, the command executes, and the application outputs information. Text interfaces use few resources, are fast and efficient to use, and generally provide responses faster than a comparable graphical application. However, a single typo can ruin your day, and text-based applications tend not to protect the user from these errors. *See also* graphical interface.

**thumbnail:** A specialized icon containing the graphical representation of the content found within a file. For example, a thumbnail image of a word processing document would contain a picture of the first page of that document. A thumbnail of an image file would contain a small representation of the image.

**tile:** A technique for displaying icons on the Start screen using rows and columns. Tiles present a number of features, such as Live Tiles — the ability to display live content. The Start screen supports two icon sizes: large (higher priority) and normal (lower priority). The large size is twice as wide as the normal size. Using tiles makes it easy to customize the interface by simply moving tiles around as needed to give them to proper position in the user's view. *See also* Live Tiles; Start screen.

**Universal Naming Convention (UNC):** A technique for naming resources that makes them easier to locate. Typically, a resource, such as a hard drive, relies on a name that's composed of server name, share name, and resource name. Each of these elements is separated by slashes or backslashes. For example, if you want the UNC name of the Windows folder in Drive C of WinServer, it appears as `\\WinServer\Drive_C\Windows`. Because of the way this naming convention works, any system needing to use the resource can use the same UNC to access it.

**Universal Serial Bus (USB):** A standardized method of connecting external components to a computer system. The USB standard defines the connectors, cables, and other elements used to make the connection between device and computer. For example, a USB connection from your camera to the computer system allows access to the pictures the camera contains. USB has gone through several standardization levels. Windows users typically have access to USB 2.0 or USB 3.0 (on newer machines).

**User Account Control (UAC):** A security protocol that monitors user access to system resources and denies access to functionality that can compromise system integrity unless the user requests elevated privileges. The UAC dialog box appears every time the user or an application requests privilege elevation. The user must affirm that the requested elevation is necessary (and desired) to perform the requested task. *See also* elevated privileges.

**Video Graphics Array (VGA):** An old, but standardized, display adapter configuration that all display adapters meet today. The VGA standard provides a bare minimum of display services and is considered the least demanding specification for a display adapter that Windows can use. Windows normally resorts to the VGA standard when it can't find a device driver for the display installed in the system. Updating a device driver allows the display adapter to provide its full functionality for displaying information onscreen. *See also* device driver.

**virtual private network (VPN):** A technique for creating a connection between two remote systems through the Internet. Normally, a VPN is used between systems that can't connect through a LAN. The use of the Internet requires the VPN to adhere to strict security requirements and to encrypt all data that passes from one machine to the next. *See also* local area network (LAN).

**ViStart:** An application originally created by LeeSoft (`http://lee-soft.com/vistart`) to replace the Start menu on Windows Vista systems. The application works well on Windows 8 systems to provide a Start menu where none exists.

**Windows Management Instrumentation (WMI):** The set of protocols and applications used to manage configuration on a Windows system. WMI provides access to information about every aspect of the Windows setup — from user configuration information to the devices that the system has installed. To provide this level of access, WMI relies on a complex database structure. Unlike most databases, WMI relies on a hierarchical format that provides the flexibility to store configuration information for all sorts of disparate needs. *See also* Windows Management Instrumentation Command line (WMIC).

**Windows Management Instrumentation Command-line (WMIC):** A console application specifically designed to access and control the WMI database. An administrator can use WMIC to perform every level of WMI task. This flexibility makes the WMIC application extremely complex, and only administrators should work with the application. *See also* Windows Management Instrumentation (WMI).

**wizard:** A specialized application for performing tasks in a step-by-step manner. A wizard breaks tasks into small, easily understood pieces and then prompts the user for input at each step. When the user has completed the wizard, the wizard has gathered the information required to perform the task and performs it for the user. Wizards help even novice users perform amazing feats on their computers.

# Index

## Apple & Mac

iPad 2 For Dummies,
3rd Edition
978-1-118-17679-5

iPhone 4S
For Dummies,
5th Edition
978-1-118-03671-6

iPod touch
For Dummies,
3rd Edition
978-1-118-12960-9

Mac OS X Lion
For Dummies
978-1-118-02205-4

## Blogging & Social Media

CityVille
For Dummies
978-1-118-08337-6

Facebook
For Dummies,
4th Edition
978-1-118-09562-1

Mom Blogging
For Dummies
978-1-118-03843-7

Twitter
For Dummies,
2nd Edition
978-0-470-76879-2

WordPress
For Dummies,
4th Edition
978-1-118-07342-1

## Business

Cash Flow
For Dummies
978-1-118-01850-7

Investing
For Dummies,
6th Edition
978-0-470-90545-6

Job Searching with
Social Media
For Dummies
978-0-470-93072-4

QuickBooks 2012
For Dummies
978-1-118-09120-3

Resumes
For Dummies,
6th Edition
978-0-470-87361-8

Starting an Etsy
Business For Dummies
978-0-470-93067-0

## Cooking & Entertaining

Cooking Basics
For Dummies,
4th Edition
978-0-470-91388-8

Wine For Dummies,
4th Edition
978-0-470-04579-4

## Diet & Nutrition

Kettlebells
For Dummies
978-0-470-59929-7

Nutrition
For Dummies,
5th Edition
978-0-470-93231-5

Restaurant
Calorie Counter
For Dummies,
2nd Edition
978-0-470-64405-8

## Digital Photography

Digital SLR Cameras &
Photography
For Dummies,
4th Edition
978-1-118-14489-3

Digital SLR Settings
& Shortcuts
For Dummies
978-0-470-91763-3

Photoshop Elements 10
For Dummies
978-1-118-10742-3

## Gardening

Gardening Basics
For Dummies
978-0-470-03749-2

Vegetable Gardening
For Dummies,
2nd Edition
978-0-470-49870-5

## Green/Sustainable

Raising Chickens
For Dummies
978-0-470-46544-8

Green Cleaning
For Dummies
978-0-470-39106-8

## Health

Diabetes For Dummies,
3rd Edition
978-0-470-27086-8

Food Allergies
For Dummies
978-0-470-09584-3

Living Gluten-Free
For Dummies,
2nd Edition
978-0-470-58589-4

## Hobbies

Beekeeping
For Dummies,
2nd Edition
978-0-470-43065-1

Chess For Dummies,
3rd Edition
978-1-118-01695-4

Drawing
For Dummies,
2nd Edition
978-0-470-61842-4

eBay For Dummies,
7th Edition
978-1-118-09806-6

Knitting
For Dummies,
2nd Edition
978-0-470-28747-7

## Language & Foreign Language

English Grammar
For Dummies,
2nd Edition
978-0-470-54664-2

French
For Dummies,
2nd Edition
978-1-118-00464-7

German
For Dummies,
2nd Edition
978-0-470-90101-4

Spanish Essentials
For Dummies
978-0-470-63751-7

Spanish
For Dummies,
2nd Edition
978-0-470-87855-2